WHAT PEOPLE ARE SAYING ABOUT
PEELING MOM OFF THE CEILING

"Every mom needs a friend like Leslie Irish Evans: a friend with a quick wit who can help you laugh through your tears of frustration; a friend who will hold your hand and not only tell you that it will all get better, but can clearly explain *how* it will all get better. In *Peeling Mom Off the Ceiling*, Leslie Irish Evans is that friend *par excellance*: funny, compassionate, and wise. With Leslie's wise guidance, her humorous stories, and her sage advice, moms will come down off the ceiling -- and back down to earth, where all the love and fun of family life truly happen."

Lauren Rosenfeld
Co-author of *Your To Be List* and *Breathing Room: The Spiritual Guide to Decluttering Your Home and Your Heart*

"If you're a Minivan Martyr, this is your wake-up call. Leslie reveals why your continual self-sacrifice is hurting you and your family and how to start enjoying those "extras" like sleep, sex, and self-esteem again."

Betsy Talbot
Author of *Strip Off Your Fear: Radiate the Confidence Within*

"Are you a confident, well adjusted, organized mom? If so, this book is not for you. Fortunately for Leslie, most of us moms do need words of support and tidbits of helpful advice in order to make it through the days, hours, and honestly sometimes the minutes that make up tending to young children. This book is chock full of the good stuff: realistic and practical musings moms need to keep themselves off the ceiling and stay grounded. Reading Leslie's wonderful book of wisdom will cost you a fraction of the price for ongoing therapy."

Nicole Knepper
Counselor/Mental Health Advocate
Author of *Moms Who Drink And Swear*

"The pressure to be a supermom has never been greater. Who can live up to those standards? Leslie packs in the tips to get over your self, get more sleep (Who doesn't need that?), and ask for help when you need it. An entertaining guide to reclaiming your personal identity while holding the world-class title of Mom."

Peg Fitzpatrick
Managing Partner of www.12Most.com

"Moms know moms best, and Leslie proves it with her hilariously accurate description of what putting on your big girl panties (of accountability) really means. This book is amazing. I could *not* put it down. Nor did I want to. Really wonderful stuff. "

Pilar Clark
www.onemommedia.com

"Being a mom is challenging. Even if you could find time for yourself, it's sometimes hard to know how to best use it. Leslie walks you through concrete ideas and practices that will help you find more space for yourself in your busy life."

Debbie Dubrow

www.DeliciousBaby.com

"Leslie's seven tips to saving your sanity are not just relevant for moms, but busy women everywhere who are trying to do it all. The plain truth is that if we women can't start making time for ourselves, asking for help, and cutting ourselves some slack, society as a whole suffers. So follow her heartfelt and delightfully cheeky advice and as you're enjoying that next relaxing massage, remember you are doing it for humanity!"

Maria Ross

Consultant, speaker and author of

Branding Basics for Small Business and *Rebooting My Brain*

PEELING MOM OFF THE CEILING

RECLAIMING YOUR LIFE FROM YOUR KIDS

For Kassia —
Take good care!
— Leslie Irish Evans

LESLIE IRISH EVANS

Poppybank Press

PEELING MOM OFF THE CEILING
RECLAIMING YOUR LIFE FROM YOUR KIDS

By Leslie Irish Evans
Poppybank Press

Published by Poppybank Press, Langley, Washington
Copyright ©2013 Leslie Irish Evans
All rights reserved.

Copyeditor: Lauren Hidden, www.HiddenHelpers.com
Cover and Interior Design: www.PearCreative.ca
Cover Copywriting: Monica Crowe, www.MonicaCroweMedia.com

Library of Congress Control Number: 2013913521
ISBN: 978-0-9897611-0-9

Printed and bound in the U.S.A

TABLE OF CONTENTS

For Mom

PREFACE

I wrote this book for 1999 Leslie.

In 1999, I was an overbusy, unhappy, lost, stressed-out suburban mommy who had an eight-year-old, a six-year-old, two cats, and a husband who worked long hours.

I fretted over my kids' homework.

I felt guilty when dinner was fast food *again*.

I had trouble sleeping and my only friends were made through my husband's work.

I knew I was Kate and Zach's mom, Chris' wife, Aladdin and Jasmine's litter-box cleaner, and ... that was it. I didn't really know who *I* was outside of those roles.

Sometimes I cried from the frustration of it all.

"You need to get a job," my husband told me (more than once).

I would usually get defensive: "I'm sorry I don't contribute to the household income, but I should get some credit for what I do around here!"

"No, no, no," he'd answer. "That's not what I mean. What I mean is, you need to get *your own thing*. You need something to do that motivates and inspires you. Something that's all yours."

I wasn't able to hear it then. I couldn't until I found my own thing that was all mine. I enrolled in massage school. My transformation began there.

Massage school was transformational not only because I now had my own thing (though that was a large part of it). It was also because I learned so much about the human body and spirit, and how stress can impact it. I learned so much about the importance of self-care, and of how relatively small habits, done consistently, can show tremendous results in our health and well-being.

At the end of this massage program, we were required to draw up a business plan. One of the tasks this involved was defining our ideal client. For me, that was easy: I wanted to work with overwhelmed, harried mothers who were taking care of everyone else and putting their own needs last. I knew a bit about that demographic.

Fast-forward a few months to my massage business, and sure enough, in they came. Those busy, stressed-out, tense suburban mommies walked through my door as crunched up and tight as rocks. *Angry* rocks. They'd leave looking transformed, and thank me profusely. What a boost to my ego! Magic hands! Look, I turned the angry rock into a beautiful maiden!

The next week, they'd come back again looking like angry rocks. And I'd massage them. And they'd relax and feel great and look completely different. This happened over and over again.

Finally, I'd had enough. "Look," I told my clients. "You can keep paying me to give you a massage and make you feel better, but shouldn't we be talking about what gets you so racked up in the first place?" It was then that I knew I wanted to start writing and speaking about stress and self-care. Especially when it came to moms. It just struck me as patently unfair that there should be so much angst and anger and frustration in such a huge part of our population.

Synchronicity being what it is, I found myself a few weeks later at a marketing workshop. The presenter told us "You need to be able to say what you do in your business *in one sentence.*" Then, of all the people in the classroom, she pointed at me: *"What do you do?"*

"I … I" she'd taken me by surprise, but I had to come up with something. *"I PEEL MOMS OFF THE CEILING!"*

She stopped in her tracks. "Oh, that's *good*," she said. "That's *a book*."

And so here we are.

LESLIE IRISH EVANS
1 August 2013

INTRODUCTION

"I think before you have kids, you can't really understand or imagine the amount of responsibility motherhood entails."

"Motherhood is a job where you NEVER get time off or vacation."

"It's still difficult to take time for myself but it is better. I guess I am from that generation where mom and wife does it all with no time for herself. This was my mother. I feel like I was caught between two different belief systems. I don't want this for my daughter."

When I had my first child, my younger sister was twenty-one years old. We attended a family wedding together when my baby was nine months old. It was eight o'clock at night, and we were walking through the lobby of a hotel.

I sighed deeply and said, "I'm *so tired.*"

My sister couldn't hide her irritation: "You had that baby *nine months ago*. How can you *still* be tired?"

A famous celebrity has twins at age 40. Four months later, we see her in a bikini on the cover of a magazine: "How Jennifer Got Back Her Pre-Pregnancy Body." Meanwhile, our hair is dirty, we're wearing a stained sweatshirt, and the waistband on our pants is still feeling awfully tight.

We're bombarded with TV commercials and magazine ads featuring smiling, trim, happy moms whose floors are shining, homes are dazzling, and whose children are polished and well-behaved.

We're tired. We're frustrated. We're misunderstood. We're lonely. And we feel like it's *our fault.*

Who profits from this pain?

1. **Not you.** Stress causes you to get sick more often. It can add on excess weight. It can trigger (or compound) chronic diseases like irritable bowel syndrome and even cancer.

2. **Not your family.** Being stressed-out can rob you of the energy to do the things you want and need to do to support your family. Unchecked stress can cause you to lash out in frustration and say things you don't really mean, damaging relationships.

3. **Not your friends.** Sure, we can say that misery loves company, but nobody likes to see their friends hurting

or suffering. Anxiety and frustration can prevent you from spending time with your friends and nurturing relationships outside of your home.

You know who benefits from "Am I a good mom?" anxiety?

Madison Avenue. Corporate America. The folks who make the floor wax and the Botox and the diet pills and the people who advertise them. These folks rely on you consistently feeling you're not good enough; that you're broken and you need fixing. That everyone else has it all figured out and you don't. *Those* folks are the ones who benefit from all of this angst and striving. ***You're paying them to continue making you feel bad.***

I've done a lot of work with moms. Stay-at-home moms. Work-outside-the-home moms. Single moms. Moms of children with special needs. They're each different and they're each the same. They are trying to figure out how to provide the best life they can for their child while trying not to lose themselves in the process (or, more often, trying to find themselves as they gave up their own dreams long ago). Women are givers. Women are nurturers. This is our great gift to the world, our strength. But sometimes we forget to turn the spigot off. We forget to refill the tank. We lose track of who we are and what we want. We forget what our own needs are and that we are individuals, too.

I once had a client who came in for a massage. She was a mother in her early thirties with two young children at home and a husband who traveled for work constantly. "How are you doing?" I asked her. She proceeded to tell me, without any trace of irony or self-awareness, how everyone else in her family was doing. How her husband was. How her son was. How her daughter was. She said nothing about herself. I pointed this out to her. "But, Mary," I asked. "How are *you*?"

She pasted a smile on her face. "Oh, I'm *fine*."

And yet she was seeing me for a massage. She had chronic neck pain that she couldn't get rid of. Are these related? You'd better believe it.

That's what we do. We paste a smile on our face and say we're *fine*. Because what choice do we have? We're the backbone of our families. If we go, the whole system falls apart, right?

If we take time for ourselves, if we stop for rest, or take "me-time," or we get ill, everything will implode, right?

Wrong.

STRESS IS A PART OF LIFE

Please note that nowhere in this book do I promise you a stress-free life. If anyone around you does, turn and run away. Why?

Because they're lying. It can't be done. Stress is an important part of life. It exists regardless of what we hope for or plan.

On a strictly biological scale, stress simply means something that causes your body to go into "fight or flight" mode (called *sympathetic* mode in medical speak). It's a very real and specific thing that causes a whole cascade of physiological responses, including an increased heart rate, dilated pupils, decreased saliva (dry mouth), and slowed digestion. Fight or flight mode absolutely has a purpose. If a lion is chasing you across the plains, you definitely want to have rapid heart rate and nice wide pupils.

The opposite of fight or flight mode is sometimes called "rest and digest" mode (*parasympathetic mode* if you want to bore people at cocktail parties). It's when our body is calm. Our heart rate slows down. Digestion increases. Our libido goes up. Life is good.

Ideally, rest and digest is our body's normal, baseline state. It's where we're calm and happy, things heal quickly, we sleep well, and all is great. But, guess what? In our modern society, it's hard to remain in this state. Work, family, coffee, noise, obligations, celebrations, deadlines, and expectations tend to put us into fight or flight mode when we don't really have anything too specific to fight or flee from. This, dear readers, is what we call *stress*.

Stress can appear in many forms, not all of them what we would typically call "bad." In the late 1960s, two guys named Holmes and Rahe developed a scale of 43 stressful life events that can contribute to people getting sick.[1] The number one stressor? Death of a spouse. That's a doozy. One hundred points. But you know what scored a fifty on the chart? Getting married. That's supposed to be a joyous occasion, right? But weddings can be hugely stressful.

Here's the point: I can't take the stress out of your life. If I could I would be sending you postcards from the South of France. **What I'm offering in this book is a way to moderate your *response* to the stress in your life through simply and consistently practicing better self-care.**

> *"Self care fills my 'tank.' I cannot care for my family with an empty tank. I have tried. Doesn't work."*

Ever had one of your kids start freaking out? Crying or having a tantrum and being completely unreasonable? And you, as their mom, knew it was because they were overtired? Or hungry? Or bored?

The stuff you're going to read in this book is stuff you already know. It's the things you naturally promote and encourage and tell your kids:

- "Oh, someone needs a nap." (Chapter Two: Preserve, Protect, and Defend Your Sleep)

- "Be sure to eat those vegetables so you're healthy." (Chapter Five: Pay Attention to What You Put In Your Body)

- "You kids are getting stir-crazy. Go outside and play." (Chapter Three: Move it and Water it)

- "Come here, Sweetie. You need a hug." (Chapter Seven: Get Touched)

The goal here is to get you to remember that **you need these things, too**. It didn't stop because you grew up. It didn't stop because you had kids. **Taking the time to make sure that you are well-rested, well-fed, well-touched, and well-exercised is not selfish.** You know what's selfish? Pursuing the egotistical fantasy of being "the perfect mom" and then becoming a burnt-out, exhausted, and resentful mess who is of no use to her family. *That's* selfish.

"I try and get a workout in at least 4 times a week, I make sure that I get a little time away from the family with my girlfriends a couple times a year, I take time to pursue some of my own interests each month (e.g. theater, music)."

HOW TO READ THIS BOOK

You can read this front to back or just hop in to the chapters that interest you. Each chapter contains the following sections:

- THE PROBLEM: Names the issue that's adding to your stress response.

- **REALITY CHECK:** This is the dope slap section. Think of it as the good friend who calls you on your bullshit.

- **THE SOLUTION:** Tips and tricks to make The Problem go away.

- **GET TO THE POINT:** No time for nuance? Brain can't retain anything other than soccer schedules? This is a summary of the chapter for those of you who can't even find time to pee in private, let alone read an entire chapter. (Though you'll be missing all my dazzling prose.)

The featured quotes in this book are real quotes from real moms who answered my surveys and questions. I'm withholding their names to respect their privacy.

Shall we begin?

CHAPTER ONE
RESIST BLACK AND WHITE THINKING

"I often really feel like a failure as a mom. I tend to have lots of 'I should haves.'"

"I fear that I will never live up to my own mother's expectations; that I'm damaging my children no matter how much I try to be a good mom."

THE PROBLEM:
Speaking and thinking about yourself in absolutes sets unreasonable expectations and is a breeding ground for guilt, disappointment, and self-loathing.

"You're the worst mother in the world!!!"

Heard that line before? Maybe with the sound of a door slamming behind it?

Or perhaps it was *you* saying those words, either aloud or silently in your own head. Maybe it was something as innocuous as letting your kid eat junk food, or maybe something more serious, like giving them a swat on the bottom when they defied your screamed orders and ran out into oncoming traffic. Whatever it was that you did, you felt bad about it, and you started mentally beating yourself up. "I'm a horrible mother," you said, either half-jokingly in front of your friends, or with a sob as you went to bed that night.

REALITY CHECK:

Get over yourself. You're not the World's Worst Mother. You're not the World's Best Mother either. Nobody keeps track of such things and even if they did, you'd still fall somewhere in the middle. You're hiding behind perfectionism because you're afraid.

You know what I don't see a whole lot of? Men fake-bragging to their friends about how they're "the World's Worst Dad." Funny how they don't make a hobby of self-deprecation the way we women do.

Some examples of black and white thinking:

- "You kids *never* listen to me!"

- "I am the *only* one who does anything around this house!"

- "I could *never* let anyone else take care of my kids because *no one* can do this job as well as I can."

It's a cop-out.

These dramatic overstatements conveniently throw us into the victim role and absolve us of having to acknowledge our own imperfection and do the hard work that goes with solving the problem. It's a perfectionist thing.

So, that was the tough love part—the bitch-slap that tells you to stop being such a drama queen. Here comes the tender part, that part that's harder for many of us to face because it makes us have to acknowledge our vulnerability:

We're scared.

We're scared that we're not up to the task. We're scared that we're going to screw up our kids. We're scared that we're going to make a misstep and something *awful* is going to happen. We're scared that we don't have our act together. We're scared that we're getting lost and that all of our own dreams and goals will never come to pass. And perhaps most of all:

We're scared that we're a BAD MOM.

It's the ultimate bugaboo, isn't it? Motherhood has become so sanctified, commodified, commercialized, and industrialized in our society that we're not really even allowed to own it anymore. It belongs to everyone ... everyone except us. We're all trying to follow the steps to a dance that has been scrutinized into oblivion. Nobody's even sure they know how to do it, but we're certain that everyone else has got it down. So you follow along, go through the motions, and hope you're ok. Because,

God forbid, someone might call you a BAD MOM if you fall out of line. (Wherever that line is.)

I'm going to only touch briefly on an even worse component to this, because it deserves its own book. (Hell, it deserves its own doctoral thesis):

"I'm always certain that the other Moms on my block look at me with disdain. That I'm that mom who doesn't know what she's doing."

Moms are each other's harshest critics.

We can blame it on Madison Avenue. We can blame it on a patriarchal society. We can blame it on religion. But the fact is this: we're hard on ourselves and we're even harder on each other.

Think about that the next time you catch yourself criticizing another mom's methods, then realize that it's this very act that causes so much of our stress and anxiety as mothers.

THE SOLUTION:

So, how do we resist this black and white thinking? How do we break the habit of thinking: *It's all-or-nothing—I'm either the World's Greatest Mom or the World's Worst Mom or The Whole World is Out to Get Me?* Here are a few steps:

OBSERVE

One of the best ways to begin changing a habit is to recognize when it shows up. Simply setting the goal of observing our behavior, without judgment, can help us on the path to changing it. In this instance, I would encourage you to start noticing your own self-talk, both external and internal.

EXTERNAL SELF-TALK

This is the stuff you actually say out-loud, to yourself or about yourself. Here's one of mine: If I botch something, I'll sometimes say out-loud "Leslie, you *dummy!*" I know another mother who will often preface statements about what she enjoys doing with "I know this is so *lame* ..." and then go on to tell me about how she likes to read history books or is staying home this Saturday night. What is the great unspoken expectation that we're failing to live up to? Should I not ever make mistakes? Should she only be interested in reading fiction or carousing every Saturday night? Probably not. But right now let's not even get into the "why." Let's just make a point to notice what we say out loud to and about ourselves.

INTERNAL SELF-TALK

This is the stuff you *think* to yourself. It can be harder to observe than the stuff we say out loud because it requires us to step outside of our own minds as we're thinking thoughts. Sometimes our thoughts don't even get to the point of words, they're more like feelings. But if we can stop and just observe what sort of internal "talk" we're giving ourselves, it can be enlightening.

HOW OTHERS TALK

Here's one we can't change directly but we can certainly change how much we are willing to engage: how are the people around us talking about themselves and other moms?

"Did you see Janet today? Late again to carpool. I'm pretty sure she was in her pajama pants, too."

"God, my son and I crashed into each other running around the corner and now he's got a black eye. Somebody's going to call Protective Services on me, I just know it!"

"Those Jackson kids are always running around the neighborhood like wild things. What is wrong with their parents?"

Sometimes we say these things jokingly. Sometimes we get into a group and we rationalize that the gossip is ok because we're really just trying to work out a problem. But here's the thing: deep down, we're scared, and we're reinforcing this police state every time we place these harsh criticisms on each other and ourselves.

UNDERSTAND THAT IT'S A PROCESS

This is not only a tip for how to resist black and white thinking; it's a tip for this entire book: It's a process.

What does that mean?

It means that you're human and you have deeply ingrained habits—nothing is going to change overnight. In fact, you may find that the niggling "black and white" voice is going to remain somewhere in your head for the rest of your life. It's not as though you're going to read these tips I offer and *BAM!* you suddenly transform into this organized, mellow person. Doesn't work that way. (If it did, this book would have cost you a LOT more money and I'd be having lunch with George Clooney.)

You will have days when you're on top of things, and days when you're not. That's how life works. Hell, I still struggle plenty with black and white thinking. But I know that over the years I've learned to loosen the reins. Let's accept that we're not perfect and …

LEARN TO LOVE THE GRAY AREAS

As a recovering perfectionist/control freak, I can tell you that only a few years ago that phrase made me feel stabby. I *hated* the gray areas.

What are gray areas? You know, those things that aren't absolute. Like that neighbor who did that horrible thing but you still remember the time when she brought you some cookies she had just made. *Is she evil or is she good?* Or that time you went on that diet to lose thirty pounds but you "only" lost eighteen. *Was the diet successful or did it fail?* Or the fact that you have mixed emotions about a policy issue. *Are you a Democrat or a Republican?* Those things that come up that don't have "pat" answers. There's complexity. There are nuances.

There's gray.

Yes or no? Up or down? Black or white? They're easier, right? Makes us not have to think so much. Eliminates wishy-washy. Handy, that. Gray is ... complicated. What shade of gray? (I assure you more than fifty exist.) Now we have to talk, compare, work it out, negotiate.

Here's how to learn to love the gray areas. Take that last sentence I just wrote in the above paragraph and change one word: Now we *get* to talk, compare, work it out, negotiate. We *get* to interact. We *get* to come to a deeper and more nuanced understanding of each other. Of ourselves. What an opportunity! That makes me smile. It didn't used to.

LAUGH AND LOVE YOURSELF

Please say the following, out loud, right now:

[laughing] <u>YOUR NAME HERE</u>, I love you!

Do it again.

I'm serious.

Did you feel your heart lighten? Did a little bit of stress go away? Even though it might have seemed silly, was there a part of you that liked hearing it? Do it again. And again. Do it until your heart remembers it.

Then, when you catch yourself engaging in black and white thinking; beating yourself up for something (you think) you did wrong, do it again. Laugh out loud and tell yourself you love yourself. Laugh because you're funny, thinking such silly things, beating yourself up. *You knucklehead!* Laugh and love as though you were your own beloved child. So serious! So *earnest!* Laugh and love that beloved child who cares *so much* about doing good. Who cares so much about being right. That's you. Love you.

LET GO OF PERFECTIONISM

Oh, thanks. Yeah, I'll just do that. Sounds super easy!

(That's what I say to my husband when I tell him I'm worried about something and he tells me "Stop worrying." Yes, I'm a very sarcastic wife.)

You bet I'll let go of perfectionism! And I will be THE BEST at it!

OK, I'll turn off the snark-o-meter for a moment and get real here. Perfectionism is deeply ingrained in a lot of us, and it's an awfully hard thing to just turn off. It comes from anxiety. It comes from expectations. I'm sure it probably gets formed from deep childhood experiences. Here's something I've learned, courtesy of life experience and from French philosopher Voltaire: *"The perfect is the enemy of the good."* When we strive for perfection, we deny ourselves the opportunity to do and create lots and lots of *good* things. Some of them *really* good.

So, when you catch yourself thinking in black and white, and you're beating yourself up and/or getting stressed out because of some perfect mom standard you're setting up for yourself, ask yourself this question:

"Do I want to be a *perfect* mom? Or do I want to be a *good* mom?"

Another take, courtesy of my own mother: "Is this *really* the hill you want to die on?" I've discovered that about 95% of the time, it's not.

GET TO THE POINT:

- Start paying attention to the things you say and think about yourself and other moms.
- Notice when you're criticizing, insulting, or setting unreasonable standards.
- Embrace your imperfect humanity.

CHAPTER TWO
PRESERVE, PROTECT, AND DEFEND YOUR SLEEP

*"I am so used to not getting enough sleep that when I do get rested,
I wonder what I did wrong."*

*"Sleep? Not quite sure how to define the loss of it once you have children. You are
awake/light sleeping when they are little, you are awake/light sleeping once they hit
the teen years. Once they become adults you may get one or two more hours of deep
sleep, but never really go to sleep for fear that they will need you."*

*"I used to make it the last priority...then I realized what a bitch I was being when I didn't
get enough sleep! It's important that I am at my best for everyone, otherwise we all
suffer. When I started making it a priority, I got so much more done and everyone
seemed so much less like a pain in the ass!"*

THE PROBLEM:
Insufficient sleep can cause mood swings, irritability, reduction of
cognitive functions, and illness.

Ahhh, sleep. That rare and precious gem. Remember when you were little and taking a nap was about the worst thing you could think of? There was too much to do and see! Who wanted a nap? Bedtime? Ugh. Ask for another glass of water. Another story. Anything but having to lie down and be still. When does that change? When we become teenagers and sleep 'til noon? College students who nap at the drop of a hat? I think it's not 'til we become moms that we really get a sense of how precious our sleep is.

I remember my mom falling asleep on the sofa in our living room fairly often, and thinking *what is her problem?*

My kids were born twenty-one months apart. I don't remember much of anything between 1993 and 1996, to be honest. I've seen pictures, though. I look *tired*. I remember praying they would nap at the same time so I could rest, too. I remember fighting against (and failing at) falling asleep on the couch while they played in the living room, hoping desperately that if one of them got hurt the other would make a noise so I'd wake up.

Do I really need to tell you how important sleep is? If you're reading this book, chances are you've lived through sleep deprivation and you know how nutsy-cuckoo you get without your sleep. But I'm going to tell you anyway, because chances are sleep is even more important than you know.

During sleep our body[2]:

- repairs damaged cells

- solves problems

- releases important hormones

- helps us process information we learned during the day

- mediates our emotions

In my practice, I would do a health intake. One of the questions I'd ask is "How's your sleep?" For most of my stressed-out mom clients, the answer was some variation of "not good."

It's sometimes a chicken and egg equation, this sleep vs. stress. In other words, when we don't get enough sleep, our stress levels increase, and when we are stressed-out, our sleep suffers. It can be a vicious cycle. But we can do some things to break the cycle.

Remember records? I'm talking actual vinyl phonograph records. The way they work is that a needle falls into a groove that's embedded into the vinyl record and picks up the sound that's recorded there. (God, it's weird that I even have to explain this.) It was always important not to scratch your records, because then the needle would follow the scratch and wouldn't play the music right. Once a record was scratched, you could never play the same song properly again.

That's what we have to do with these bad habits we've established. We repeat them over and over again until the grooves are very deep and it's hard for the needle to follow anything else. What we have to do is scratch the hell out of that habit-record so that we can't play it the same anymore.

> ## REALITY CHECK:
> You are not "one of those people who doesn't need much sleep." Studies are increasingly showing that just about everyone needs seven to eight hours of sleep each night and if you're not getting that, you're compromising your health.

Moms of newborns? You get a pass here. Sleep when you can. Unless you have outside help or are blessed with a naturally sleepy baby, you won't be able to get a good night's sleep for a few months, at least. Sorry.

THE SOLUTION:

It starts with better hygiene.

No, I'm not calling you stinky. In this case, we're talking about *sleep hygiene.* Hygiene means *conditions or practices conducive to health.*[3] When we establish sleep-inducing habits, we're practicing good sleep hygiene. (See the Resources section for more information on improving your sleep.)

"I'm very good at putting my kids to bed. I'm not very good
at all at putting myself to bed."

Bingo.

You know, here's the funny thing about this book. If you look at what I'm espousing here: get good sleep, get good exercise, eat nutritious food, ask for help, etc., it's all stuff we resolutely pursue for our kids. We know how important this stuff is, that's why we monitor it like crazy in our kids' lives. But we forget to hold ourselves to the same standard.

So, how are you at putting yourself to bed? I'm going to show you a common scenario.. Tell me if this seems familiar:

You've got a big day planned tomorrow. Lots to do. Maybe you have a big presentation at work. Maybe you've got three different doctor appointments for the kids. Maybe you're leaving for vacation the next day. You know you want to get a good night's sleep so that you will be ready to tackle your big day tomorrow. You say to yourself: *I'm going to bed at 9:30.* 9:30 arrives. You might even notice it and think *Ah, ok, it's 9:30. Time for bed.* But … you decide you're going to check that email one more time. Which leads you to a link to a funny cat video. Which leads you to an article about something. Which leads you to … the next thing you know, it's 11p.m. *Damn it!* You meant to go to bed ninety minutes ago! *What happened?*

SET AN ALARM CLOCK FOR BEDTIME

You've already got an alarm clock. One that wakes you up in the morning. Here's a wacky idea: What if you also set one for *bedtime*? It can be a great way to "train" yourself to get ready for bed. And that's what this is, you know. Training. You've probably got a bedtime routine for your children, right? (Or you did when they were little.) Maybe bath, pajamas, brush teeth, story time, lights out. This is what we need to start doing for ourselves. Bedtime routines. We have this tendency to just keep trying to cram more stuff in (Reading! Internet! Housework!) until we're exhausted, then hope that sleep somehow finds us.

Set an alarm for an established bedtime then stick to it. Because it's all well and good to say "Oh, yes, I will set an alarm to go off at 10 p.m. to remind me to go to bed" but if we still do the "right after I check my email, get these dishes done, start a fight with my husband" then we have **ignored our own boundaries and we train ourselves that we don't really mean what we say.**

PAY ATTENTION TO YOUR CAFFEINE INTAKE

I love caffeine. I live in Seattle, and you can't swing a dead cat without hitting a decent espresso stand. (I love that expression. "Swing a dead cat." Where the hell did it come from? Was swinging dead cats a *thing* at some point?) We have lots of gray days here, and we have darn good coffee to keep us humming. And hum we do. Sometimes too much. Most of us know that caffeine can keep us awake, but some of us might not know exactly how much. People have varying levels of sensitivity to caffeine, and it's my strong impression that some people misjudge their caffeine sensitivity.

Example: Susan was undergoing a great deal of stress. She had recently broken up with her boyfriend of two years, plus she had experienced sexual harassment in her workplace and was dealing with the aftermath of bringing the incident to the attention of her supervisors. So, as you can imagine, she was really stressed out. Legit reasons for stress, to be sure. As we sat down and did her health intake, I asked her how her sleep was. "Not good," she said. "I don't sleep well at all." I then asked her about her caffeine consumption. This woman was regularly taking in several servings of caffeine a day. Two large cups of coffee in the morning, two diet colas at lunch, and at least two highly caffeinated energy drinks in the afternoon. Now, as I said, people's tolerance for caffeine can vary widely, but I know for me if I were to have that much caffeine, I would NOT be able to sleep. (I would also probably crap my pants. Caffeine is a powerful bowel stimulant.) I gently suggested that she consider dialing back on the caffeine. "No caffeine after 1 p.m." is a rule I often find helpful.

I'd love to end this story telling you she took my advice and everything got better, but I can't. Susan was *not* happy with this advice, and never came back to see me. People often find a difference between what they need to do and what they're willing to do. This woman wanted me to "fix" her but didn't want to take responsibility for her own health. That's a recipe for failure.

BE CAREFUL ABOUT ALCOHOL

We've all heard of a "nightcap," right? A drink before bedtime, ostensibly to help you sleep. I know of plenty of people who adhere to this rule. A glass of wine to help them relax. But be careful. Alcohol can help you fall asleep. But alcohol can also affect how well you stay asleep. Specifically, studies have shown it decreases the REM (Rapid Eye Movement) stage of our sleep, which is when our body does most of its repair and rejuvenation. This sleep occurs mostly in the second half of the night.[4]

I'm sorry to say I've run up against resistance here, too. I told a client who was drinking three glasses of wine before bed and complaining about her sleep patterns that it was quite possibly the wine that was interfering. She didn't want to hear it. "I don't *want* to stop drinking wine before bed," she complained. Oookay. But understand that cause and effect occurs regardless of whether we want it to or not.

So we've looked at setting an alarm for bedtime. We've checked our caffeine and alcohol consumption. We've established rules for good sleep hygiene. And we still don't feel like we're getting as much sleep as we should. What now?

CONSIDER USING A WHITE NOISE MACHINE

When our kids are small, a lot of us develop a keen ear at nighttime. We sleep "with one ear open" in case our child needs us. It's a bit of an anxiety thing, trying to anticipate problems. Then, when the child does call out for us, we've validated the anxiety. This scenario is understandable and even necessary for small children. But for an awful lot of moms (me included), sleeping with one ear open doesn't shut off once the kids are older. We've trained ourselves to be light sleepers and to jump at any possible noise. For this I suggest using a white noise machine.

When sound waves extend over a wide range of frequencies, it tends to make a "blanket" of sound, a dull roar or shushing sound. This is known as *white noise.* Think of the ocean's quiet roar or the sound a fan makes when it's on all the time. This background noise can often help to cover up more singular noises around it. This can be really helpful for those of us who've trained ourselves to listen for being needed.

A white noise machine is one that's designed to create that white noise or shushing sound. Some can make the sound of the ocean or the sound of rain. I prefer one that makes a fairly loud roar. It's very helpful for covering up the little hiccups, knocks, and dings that happen at night but don't really need our attention. (See the Resources section for info on white noise machines.)

CHANGE YOUR EXPECTATIONS AROUND SLEEP

Are your sleep expectations realistic?

I was doing a radio show about sleep and I contacted my cousin. She has four children fairly close in age, and I wondered what her sleep situation was like. Here's what she told me:

> *"I had to change my expectations of sleep. I have four young kids, and they keep me very busy. There was simply no way I was going to sleep like I did, say, in college. Once I accepted that fact and stopped holding myself to that ridiculous standard it got a lot easier."*

This fascinated me. I simply hadn't thought of it. She was right. Are you doing that? I was. I was holding myself to the standard of when I got the most sleep in my life. College. I slept for nine hours a day in college. (Not necessarily in a row.) *To have it set in my head that this was still the proper standard for sleep even though I was now a thirty-year-old woman with two young children was setting myself up for disappointment and resentment.* Maybe we aren't meant to get that much sleep at this point in our lives.

I say this not to mitigate all of the other things I posted here. Sleep is wildly important for you health and well-being. But reasonable expectations are important, too. Keep that in mind, won't you?

GET TO THE POINT:

- Set an alarm for your bedtime.
- Monitor your caffeine and alcohol intake.
- Consider a white noise machine.
- Check your expectations around sleep.

CHAPTER THREE
MOVE IT AND WATER IT

"I wish I exercised more. I know I need more. But, usually I have to make a choice with my time and 'I' don't normally win! "

"Mother to young kids combined with being a nursing student equals not a lot of free time. And the small amount of down time usually sees me too exhausted to do much of anything."

"Sadly, heavy sighing does not count as regular physical activity. Although I do believe frustration and anger should count for some cardio."

THE PROBLEM:
Lack of regular physical activity combined with poor hydration makes us tired, irritable, and contributes to long-term poor health.

In 2005, I was hard at work in massage school, earning my certificate. One of the requirements we had for school was to perform an "externship" giving massage in a setting other than the school. I chose to work with elders in a retirement facility. It was one of the most rewarding experiences of my massage education. The community I worked with ranged from seniors living independently in the apartments to those requiring intensive round-the-clock nursing care, and all of those in between. Some days I worked in the nursing facility, giving gentle shoulder rubs to wheelchair-bound residents. Other days I worked at the apartments, doing full massages for the more active residents.

The massages I gave at the apartments weren't really any different from the ones we gave each other at school, as these residents were understood to be healthy and able-bodied. But we did do a health intake as a) should be done for all massage clients and b) c'mon, these people were in their 80s. One particular client, I'll call her "Mrs. Gustafson," was 89 years young. I generally hate that phrase, "She's _____ years young". It's way too cutesy for my taste. But if I told you she was 89 years old, you'd get entirely the wrong impression. She had a sharp mind and could have passed for someone twenty years younger. After I did the intake and determined that a massage would be just fine for her, I gave her the usual instructions to disrobe, get on the massage table under the sheets, and I'd be back in. I then left the room.

After several minutes, I knocked on the door. "Mrs. Gustafson? Are you ready?" No answer. Uh-oh. I knocked again. "Mrs. Gustafson?" Well, perhaps she didn't hear me. I opened the door. There, naked as a jaybird and attempting to climb onto the massage table, was Mrs. Gustafson.

Now, you need to understand something: though we deal with naked clients nearly all of the time, we almost never see anything untoward. We have strict ethical guidelines in the massage profession: We leave the room when clients are disrobing, ask them to get under the sheets, then return once they're ready. We keep private areas draped at all times. We leave the room when we're done, allowing the client to get dressed in privacy. We really don't see anything.

"Well, it doesn't matter," said Mrs. Gustafson, acknowledging my presence but continuing to struggle into the bed. "I guess you've seen it all, huh?"

I have now, I thought. The ethical thing to do at this point was to help my elderly client onto the table, which I proceeded to do. We went on to have a successful massage.

Why am I telling you this story? Not to make fun of an old lady. I'm telling you this because Mrs. Gustafson was in great shape. Her skin was clear. Her mind was clear. She looked *terrific.* Many of the clients that I saw in that room looked terrific. And while my experience hardly constitutes a scientific survey, here's what they all had in common:

They all got regular exercise, and they all drank plenty of water.

MOVE IT

"I haven't always been great about exercising but in the last year I've noticed that I makes a HUGE impact on how well I handle everyday situations. I'm calmer and happier and more productive, so I'm learning to make it a priority."

Our bodies were made for moving. Walking, dancing, reaching up, bending over, running, jumping, squatting, lunging. When we were running around on the Serengeti millennia ago, these activities were required of us. Nowadays ... not so much. Even a mere one hundred years ago we still had to do a lot more than we do now. Automation and innovation are wonderful, don't get me wrong. You probably wouldn't be reading this book otherwise, but while it has given us much more time for enrichment, it has made our bodies grow stiff and sore.

I want to stress a really important note here. When I talk about moving your body, I'm talking about just that. Yes, I mean exercise, but I think people have gotten really hung up on that word in this day and age. To many, exercise means playing a sport or going to a gym and working themselves into an aggressive, raging sweat. A time and a place exist for that, but I'm broadening this scope to mean so much more than that. I mean, simply: Move. Your. Body.

I regularly asked my massage clients what they did for movement activity. I asked them this specifically so I could have an idea of where their body was likely to be more tight, and less tight. For example: People who walk regularly are likely to have tight hips. Softball players might have tender shoulders. Gardeners have tight backs.

"Movement activity?" they would ask, looking puzzled.

"Y'know, how do you move during the day?"

Still puzzled.

OK, fine, I'll say it: "Exercise?"

The light bulb would appear over their heads, and then almost instantly a guilty expression would come over their face. "Oh, I don't exercise like I should."

Damn it, this is the thing I was trying to avoid. Guilt trips don't help anybody. Especially massage clients who are coming to me to reduce stress!

So, here's the thing. When I ask you to "Move your body," I'm not talking about training for the Olympics. I'm not talking about running a marathon. (Unless that's what you want to do, in which case I say GO FOR IT. I will watch you from the sidelines, while eating a cupcake.) I'm talking about, literally, moving your body. Stretching, jumping, dancing, twisting, walking ... anything that gets you up and moving around. NOT so that you'll lose weight (though that is entirely possible), but for the following reasons.

REGULAR PHYSICAL ACTIVITY [5]

- Controls your weight

- Reduces your risk of cardiovascular disease

- Reduces your risk for Type 2 diabetes and metabolic syndrome

- Reduces your risk for some cancers

- Strengthens your bones and muscles

- Improves your mental health and mood

- Improves your ability to do daily activities and prevents falls

- Increases your chances of living longer

Oh, and most important? It improves sleep and reduces stress. Hello! Isn't that why you picked this book up in the first place?

> *"I can see a significant improvement in my mood, outlook, and tolerance when I have been able to exercise that day."*

Here's another big motivator for moving your body: Recent studies are showing that being sedentary is *awful* for your health. A study in Australia measured how much television people watched. When they controlled all other factors, they learned that every hour you spend being sedentary takes 21.8 minutes off of your life. By comparison, a single cigarette takes off 11 minutes.[6] By that measure, **being sedentary is twice as bad for you as smoking.**

REALITY CHECK:

You don't have time NOT to exercise. This isn't about losing weight or fitting in to a bikini, it's about your health and your longevity.

THE SOLUTION:

MOVE YOUR BODY – HOW TO DO IT

Don't have a regular exercise habit? Don't want one? Here are some tips for how to move your body more.

1) MULTI-TASK – Now, normally, I'm against multi-tasking. As my friend Debbie Rosemont says, "Multi-tasking makes you stupid."[7] But here I'm willing to make an exception. Sometimes we have to trick our minds in order to get what we want. So, try squeezing

in movement while you're doing something else. Like to watch TV at night? Instead of skipping past the commercials, skip *during* the commercials. March in place. Do some pushups. Or dance around the living room to the commercial jingles. When the show comes back on, you get to sit back down. While you're brushing your teeth, do some stretches. Hoist a leg up on the counter and do a stretch while you brusha-brusha. After a few weeks, you'll be surprised at how much farther your leg will go.

I wrote a great deal of this book at a treadmill desk. It's a desk that's built up over a treadmill, which I walk on very slowly (1 mph) as I type (It's too hard to type if I'm going any faster than that). Not a heart-pounding workout by any means, but that's exactly the point. Instead of sitting perfectly still and being almost completely sedentary while I'm on my computer, I'm now gently and consistently moving my body. (Details about the treadmill desk in the Resources section at the end of this book.)

2) ACT LIKE A KID – A *little* kid. They run. They jump. They dance. They climb. They *move*. Afraid you'll look weird? Do it anyway.

A famous story has early 20th century athlete Jim Thorpe deciding to follow a toddler around, doing everything the toddler did exactly as he did it, for as long as he could. Jim Thorpe was a famous and multi-talented athlete, who played pro football and won Olympic Gold Medals in the decathlon and pentathlon. Many called him "the Greatest Athlete of the 20th Century." As the story goes, he dropped from exhaustion after four hours. The tot kept going.

3) CLEAN YOUR HOUSE – Stand down, this isn't me trying to trick you! Here's something cool I learned: Housework counts as exercise. Seriously.

I got this really cool device called a FitBit. I wear it on my wrist like a bracelet. It monitors my physical activity, and thus how many calories I burn in a day. It shows a running count on a graph on my computer. That graph is the coolest part. *Some* calories are always being burned. (Even sleeping your body is still burning energy, just not very much.) If I go for a run, a spike is created in the chart, but guess where I also saw spikes (i.e. extra calories burned) in a given day? When I was doing housework. Not as big and grand as the ones when I went for a brisk walk, mind you, but they were definitely there. Doing dishes, vacuuming, dusting, picking up toys—they all showed as activity spikes on the readout. You know what DIDN'T show up as an activity spike? Sitting in front of my computer. In fact, it showed exactly the same as "sleeping" did on my graph. AUGH! DO you know how much time I sit in front of a computer? A lot. As far as my body is concerned … I'm asleep. (For science's sake, I also wore my FitBit during sex. I'm not going to tell you what the graph said—but let's just say I might need to put more effort into some things in my life.) So, take heart. You don't have to join a gym or run a marathon. You just need to move. And housework *counts*. (see Resources section for more info on the FitBit)

4) GET A DOG – Especially a puppy who's not potty trained yet. You'll be out walking that beast several times a day. Guess what? You both reap the benefits.

WATER IT

ON WATER:

"I've dubbed myself 'Human Hummingbird.' I need a sweet drink, and water is only for toilets. (Kidding, but you get the idea). … I wish I could say, 'I drink water because I want to show my kids that is the healthy choice,' but I've created four little hummingbirds, just like me."

In my massage practice, I joked about implementing the following: I would tape a quarter to a card, put a gold star on it and give it to my clients who were good about drinking water. The quarter was to pay them back for the money they saved me on massage oil . Seriously, I had to use much less oil on people who drank a lot of water. Their skin was soft and well-hydrated, so it didn't soak up as much oil as a dehydrated person's would. Water also helps muscles stay nice and plump and supple. When massaging a person who's very dehydrated, their muscles feel like modeling clay. You can squeeze them and they don't really bounce back. A hydrated person's muscle feels supple and springy.

So, why should you care? Who cares if I have to use more oil or what the muscles feel like?

Here's why. Besides the esthetic benefits of clear, soft skin, water is what your body needs to perform at its best. I'm going to take us down to the very cellular level of our bodies right now for a brief lesson in cell hydration.

Picture a cell. One cell of your body. Now billions upon billions of cells are in your body, and I won't get into the details of how cells are classified, just know this: On the most basic level, a cell is a cell is a cell. Regardless of what they do in your body, the physiology of a cell is basically the same: It takes nutrients in, and it poops waste out. Just like you! OK, I'm not sure we can say a cell actually poops, but it does excrete waste.

Picture a balloon filled with water. Now imagine that balloon has a mouth, and an anus. (Yes, I just asked you to imagine a balloon with an anus, welcome to Leslie's World.) Now inside that water balloon imagine a few little charms floating around. Maybe one looks like a monkey, one is a car, one looks like a fish. Each of those charms has a job to do. The monkey's job is to eat all the carbs that come into the cell, the car's job is to create energy and go, and the fish's job is to eat up the protein that comes into the cell. They need to swim all around in that water balloon to do their job.

Now imagine the water balloon, instead of being filled with nice clear water, was filled with custard.

It would be MUCH harder for the charms to swim around and do what they needed to do, right? It would also be harder for the water balloon to take in the nutrients it needed through its mouth and probably harder to flush out the wastes. Things would just be all sluggish.

This is what every cell in your body does. It's like a water balloon that needs to eat and excrete, and the "charms" are the organelles that utilize fuel and create energy. If they don't have a well-hydrated medium to float around in, it's harder for them to do their job. The result is dehydration, and it can manifest in all sorts of ways: headaches, thirst, constipation, fatigue, dizziness, and more.

Make sense? This is why you need water. Not to lose weight or have soft, clear skin. Those are just side benefits. You need to drink enough water so that your cells, which make up *all of the systems of your body*, are able to do their work as efficiently and cleanly as possible.

How much water should you drink? People argue about this all the time. Six to eight 8-ounce glasses is a number you will hear often, and I think it's a good guideline to shoot for. You'll notice increased urination, at first. This fact often puts people off who are trying to increase their water intake. Your body will adjust. It's a combination of your body shedding the excess water weight it was hoarding and your bladder not being used to quite so much fluid. Trust me, after a few days it gets better.

You can drink *too much* water. It's a situation called hypernatremia and it basically happens when you drink too much plain water and wash too many electrolytes out of your system. You've either got to be an endurance athlete performing very strenuous exercise and sweating a lot while drinking plain water or a knucklehead trying to win some sort of contest and drinking as much water as you can. Either way, you've got to work at it, but it's possible. Please don't do that.

HOW TO DRINK MORE WATER:

1. Set up a drinking cup at every sink in your house. Every time you use that sink, drink a cup of water.

2. Buy a big 48-64 oz. reusable water bottle. In the morning, fill 'er up. Try to finish it before 6pm (so you're not up peeing all night).

3. Don't like the taste of water? Add lemon slices, cucumber slices, mint, and/ or ginger.

4. Technically, any non-caffeinated beverage can count as your water. (Fruit juice, diet soda, herbal tea, etc.) Even caffeinated beverages can count, according to some people (caffeine is a diuretic, which means it causes your body to excrete more water, but some argue the amount isn't proportional to the fluid intake). Because of the different additives and/or calories and/or effects of beverages that aren't water, I tend to still try to do 6-8 cups of real water and not count the other ones.

Sound like too much trouble? Here's what I advocate: Just try it. Use yourself as a guinea pig. Set aside *one week* where you will focus on drinking eight glasses of water a day and see what results. Did you drop a few pounds? (Hydration prevents water bloat). Did your skin clear up? Did you have more energy? (Dehydration can lead to fatigue.) Or did you just pee a lot and not notice any difference? Mrs. Gustafson knows the benefits, and she kept at it. Looking good, Mrs. Gustafson!

GET TO THE POINT:

- Being sedentary is worse for your health than smoking.
- Don't stress about getting a big "workout," just move your body more throughout the day. Try to reduce the amount of time you sit.
- Your body's trillions of cells need water to function properly.
- Keep water handy around the house and drink more to improve your energy and overall health.

CHAPTER FOUR
MAKE ROOM FOR SPIRIT

"I take time to talk to my God every night as I am going to sleep. I would like to be more engaged with my church community, but I don't make the time."

"It's hard to separate spirit from religion. I'm an atheist so I don't practice/use spirit."

THE PROBLEM:
Overscheduled lives and "the daily grind" can leave us feeling isolated and unfulfilled.

Are you a scheduler? Do you have a day planner, or an app on your phone that lets you schedule your day? That's comforting, isn't it? Seeing the day all mapped out. Wake at 7. Lunch at noon. Pick up the kids at 3. How scheduled are you? Do you schedule your entire day completely, or just the important stuff? Oh, and here's an even better question: What counts as "important" stuff? We make room in our lives for the stuff we think is important. Do you make room for spirit?

I think, for starters, we'd better define "spirit." Philosophers, learned scholars, clergy, and laypeople have been trying to define spirit for millennia. I'm going to do it right here in this humble little book in one sentence (I'm treading carefully and specifically, here. This can be a tricky topic because for many, spirit comes deeply bundled with religion, and for the sake of inclusivity and commonality I am teasing out the spirit part as a stand-alone. Stay with me here. There's room for all.):

Spirit is the part of you that exists as part of a greater, external whole.

Whoa.

Your mileage may vary, but that's the definition of spirit I'm sticking to here for the purposes of this discussion. *It's the part of you that belongs to something bigger.*

OK, so what does *that* mean?

Human beings are social creatures. We were meant to live in community: with each other, with nature, with *something*. One of the cruelest and most difficult punishments we can give to another human being is solitary confinement. No interaction with humans, or the sky, or trees, or water, or even, in some cases, light. It's the opposite of how we were meant to exist, and it can crush people. When we can live in community, in relationship to something or someone, that's when we thrive.

One of the things I've noticed about modern motherhood (at least in the Western world) is how very isolating it can become. In earlier times, we all lived near our extended families for our entire lives. There were sisters, grandmothers, aunts, cousins who all helped us out and helped us to raise our children. Now with our fast, mobile culture it's not at all unusual for grown children to move far away from where they were raised to pursue a career. It certainly happened in my family. I was born and raised in Michigan, but when my husband and I got married, it was a matter of following him around the country (to Boston, then San Francisco, then finally Seattle) as his career advanced. And each time we moved, my circle of support and "community" had to be built from scratch all over again. After a certain number of moves (there were additional moves within the areas described as well) I was mostly reliant on my young children and my never-home husband for my sense of community. I began to lose my sense of self and my identity. Who was I? A good friend at that time said, "Leslie, you need to find your *tribe*."

A tribe. A community. Something we belong to. Something that is bigger than us. Because when we are in the midst of modern motherhood, it's so easy to get completely swept up in the minutiae of our busy little lives. We think we're alone. Spirit says we're not.

So it's with this definition and this understanding that I encourage you to make room for spirit. Because if we load up our day with busy work (carpools, projects, activities, perfectionism) it can be really easy to start feeling like we're running the whole show and that the world is going to fall apart without us keeping our hands in everything. We forget that, deep down, we actually have very little control over how life will unfold.

"I think it is really important to share your beliefs in spirit with your children. Not so that they believe the same things, but so that they realize that even the all-powerful Mommy knows that some things are beyond even her wisdom."

REALITY CHECK:

Regardless of your thoughts on religion, faith, science, or nature, you are a spiritual being. You have to make regular room for peace in your life for your own spiritual health.

So how do we "make room for spirit," and what do we do once we have?

THE SOLUTION:

MAKE USE OF WHITE SPACE

White space (also known as *negative space*) is a graphic arts concept. It basically describes the space that is NOT being used by the artist's medium. For example, the page you're reading this on right now: any part of it that's not covered with ink (or dark pixels) is the white space. It's the space not being used. Even though we might not give that unused space much thought, it has an impact on how we receive the work. In short, more white space equals more calm. Not buying it? Note the "feeling" you get from the next two pages:

PEACE

PEACE PEACE PEACE PEACE PEACE PEACE PEACE
PEACE PEACE PEACE PEACE PEACE PEACE PEACE
PEACE PEACE PEACE PEACE PEACE PEACE PEACE
PEACE PEACE PEACE PEACE PEACE PEACE PEACE
PEACE PEACE PEACE PEACE PEACE PEACE PEACE
PEACE PEACE PEACE PEACE PEACE PEACE PEACE
PEACE PEACE PEACE PEACE PEACE PEACE PEACE
PEACE PEACE PEACE PEACE PEACE PEACE PEACE
PEACE PEACE PEACE PEACE PEACE PEACE PEACE
PEACE PEACE PEACE PEACE PEACE PEACE PEACE
PEACE PEACE PEACE PEACE PEACE PEACE PEACE
PEACE PEACE PEACE PEACE PEACE PEACE PEACE
PEACE PEACE PEACE PEACE PEACE PEACE PEACE
PEACE PEACE PEACE PEACE PEACE PEACE PEACE
PEACE PEACE PEACE PEACE PEACE PEACE PEACE
PEACE PEACE PEACE PEACE PEACE PEACE PEACE
PEACE PEACE PEACE PEACE PEACE PEACE PEACE
PEACE PEACE PEACE PEACE PEACE PEACE PEACE
PEACE PEACE PEACE PEACE PEACE PEACE PEACE
PEACE PEACE PEACE PEACE PEACE PEACE PEACE
PEACE PEACE PEACE PEACE PEACE PEACE PEACE
PEACE PEACE PEACE PEACE PEACE PEACE PEACE
PEACE PEACE PEACE PEACE PEACE PEACE PEACE
PEACE PEACE PEACE PEACE PEACE PEACE PEACE
PEACE PEACE PEACE PEACE PEACE PEACE PEACE
PEACE PEACE PEACE PEACE PEACE PEACE PEACE
PEACE PEACE PEACE PEACE PEACE PEACE PEACE
PEACE PEACE PEACE PEACE PEACE PEACE PEACE
PEACE PEACE PEACE PEACE PEACE PEACE PEACE
PEACE PEACE PEACE PEACE PEACE PEACE PEACE
PEACE PEACE PEACE PEACE PEACE PEACE PEACE
PEACE PEACE PEACE PEACE PEACE PEACE PEACE
PEACE PEACE PEACE PEACE PEACE PEACE PEACE
PEACE PEACE PEACE PEACE PEACE PEACE PEACE

Big difference, right? The first page is quietly powerful. One word. LOTS of white space. The second page has the exact same word on it, but it's so busy and cluttered that our brain nearly buzzes with overwhelm. It's not just words, it's anything. Lots of white space equals calm.

So it goes with getting in touch with spirit. It's much harder to get in touch with that quietly powerful part of you that belongs to something greater in the midst of chaos. You need to put that pause in there—that unused white space—to allow it to flourish.

Let's take the white space concept to your daily schedule. Whether you keep a literal schedule that contains a graphic representation of how you spend your time, or you keep it all in your head, are there gaps in that schedule? That's where we make room for spirit. What? You have everything scheduled up to your teeth? Other demands or responsibilities eat up any open time in your schedule? This is where we learn to respect our own white space and hold it for ourselves.

If you haven't got white space in your calendar, make some. Pick a specific time … let's start with, say, an hour on a Tuesday afternoon. Let's say 2 p.m. It goes like this: On this particular Tuesday afternoon, from 2 p.m. to 3 p.m., you will block off this time on your calendar and *you will not schedule anything during this time.* When 2 p.m. on Tuesday arrives, *you will then, and only then, decide what you want to do that will nurture your spirit.* Do you want to go for a walk? Would you like to read a book? How 'bout a nice warm bath? Maybe you'll sit down and listen to an entire album of music in one go. Or, perhaps, you'll sit and do absolutely nothing but listen to your own breathing.

Here's what you may NOT do: household chores, catch up on work, or anything else that qualifies as a "should." You also may not plan what you're going to do with this time beforehand. You must decide when the moment arrives what you feel would be most nurturing to you.

Are you twitching yet? This is hard stuff! Especially for moms who are constantly striving for ways to get *more* done, to be *more* efficient. This is a fingernail on the chalkboard for us Type-A planners. *What do you mean we're going to set aside some time just to pay attention to spirit and we can't plan it out ahead?*

Here's what's likely to happen: we'll see that blank time there on the schedule, and we'll give it away. *Oh, you need me to come in and help with your classroom? You need me Tuesday at 2 p.m.? Uh, no, I don't have anything planned.* (In our brain we're thinking *I'll just move that "make room for spirit" hour to another time.*) It's not really that important, right? We can do it later.

But we don't. This is what got us up on that ceiling in the first place. We give parts of ourselves away over and over, thinking we can get it back, but we don't. We forget how to hang on to what is *ours*.

Once you've played with white space a bit, try moving it from something you do weekly to something you do daily. It doesn't really matter how long the time is (though more *is* better.) What's more important is that you make it a regular practice.

BREATHE

In many languages, *spirit* literally means *breath*. (Latin: *spiritus*. Hebrew: *ruach* Greek: *pneuma*) and the act of sitting with and listening to your breath is a great way to allow spirit into your life. If we go with our definition of spirit being that part of you that exists as a greater external whole, think about it in terms of your breath. When you breathe in, you are taking in the air and the atmosphere of the world around you. That's a whole big atmosphere, of course, circling the entire globe. Part of it, every time you inhale—a little tiny part of it, but a part that is *vital* to you—is going inside of you and transforming you. And when you exhale, a different, transformed, little tiny part of it is going back into the atmosphere, and changing that. Pretty amazing, right? So you sit, and you breathe, and you take in the world, and you give back to the world. That is spirit. And when you do this, you will find your stress levels going down. Your blood pressure will lower. Your muscular tension will decrease. "Interrupt stress often" says noted reflexologist Kevin Kunz. This is one way to interrupt stress. It's self-soothing.

GET OUTSIDE

"Taking time to get outside or meditate or just have 'me time' helps me feel good."

It's easy to live in your head. In your room. In your house. If you think about a disconnect from spirit as feeling apart from any sort of greater, external whole, then it seems like isolating yourself indoors, in layer upon layer of rooms, is a great way to do it. Why do business executives argue over who gets the window office? Because to spend all day in a windowless room is spirit-draining. Connecting yourself with the outdoors is another easy and obvious way to see, feel, and be a part of a greater, external whole. You, the trees, the birds, and the bugs are all there together, sharing in the benefits of the sun, the wind, and the rain. It's restorative. When you are out in nature, you can *receive*. Stuck inside with the kids all day, you can be sucked dry. "Mom, I need this." "Mom, can you do that?" and that's just the kids, not to mention the laundry and the dishes and all of the things your home asks of you. Outside in nature, you can replenish. Take the sun. Take the fresh air. They're for you, and the only thing they ask in return is that you breathe.

GET TO THE POINT:

- Build "white space" (unscheduled time) into your daily schedule to give yourself time to recharge.
- Take time to sit and focus on your breath.
- Get outside. Nature is soothing to the spirit.

CHAPTER FIVE
PAY ATTENTION TO WHAT YOU PUT IN YOUR BODY

"Food is: My friend. My enemy. My lover. My identity. As "She Who Feeds People", it's the way I express love."

"I try to be aware and conscientious, but time and responsibilities get in the way."

THE PROBLEM:
What we eat and drink, and how we feel about what we eat and drink, can have a tremendous impact on our health and sense of well-being.

Here it is. The eating chapter. Is there a topic more fraught for women than this? I'm not sure there is. I'm going to tread carefully here and hope that something connects for you.

I think I first learned of the delicacy of this topic in college. I lived in an all-female co-op house on campus. This meant that all of the inhabitants were responsible for the food and cleaning inside (as opposed to dorms, which had maintenance staff and a cafeteria). I was the Food Manager, which meant I was responsible for planning the meals and purchasing the food for the house. I liked this job because I enjoyed the challenge of planning meals and it got me out of having to scrub the toilets.

I quickly learned that in a house of thirty college-aged women, there were at least thirty different histories, tastes, stories, peccadilloes, hang-ups, and outright disorders to take into consideration. Jane couldn't handle even a hint of spiciness. Mary was bulimic, and would hoard any and all graham crackers I bought for the house. Many of them didn't know how to cook. Some were vegetarian. Others wouldn't touch a vegetable if you paid them. (OK, that's hyperbole. They were all poor college students, they *totally* would have done it if you'd paid them.) I had really only dealt with my family before this, and we all knew what we liked so there hadn't been too much fuss.

As I've chatted with various women on this topic, a very interesting point always comes up: Their relationship with food is *intrinsically* connected to their body image. For a great many of us, food equals weight. And because of that, food also often equals guilt.

We've got a really messed up relationship with food, body image, and pleasure in our culture. It's a far bigger topic than I could ever hope to tackle in this book, so I won't, but it must at least be acknowledged. Also, it drives me crazy.

Go out to lunch with a bunch of women (I'm sorry, my sisters, but I almost never see men do this) and watch what happens when the waiter brings the dessert tray around. Eyes are riveted, and then the demurrals kick in:

> "Oh, I shouldn't."

> "Well, maybe just a bite."

> "Oh, let's split one."

I have no problem with monitoring what one eats, in fact, it's a big part of what this chapter is about. But self-flagellation is a whole different thing:

> "Oh, this is so sinful!"

> "Oh my God, get this away from me. I can't believe I'm still eating it!"

> "I feel so guilty."

IF YOU FEEL GUILTY, THEN DON'T EAT IT.

Ever been to France? I have. Many times. I love France. And here's one of the big things I love about France: *They take deep pleasure in their food and they don't feel an ounce of guilt about it.* Food is meant to be enjoyed, and they do.

This chapter is called *Pay Attention to What You Put In Your Body*, and I chose these words carefully. It has to do with taking responsibility for the food choices we make. To mindlessly shove whatever's most convenient into our bodies on a regular basis is to set ourselves up for health problems. Please note: I AM NOT JUST TALKING ABOUT GETTING FAT. In fact, I'm trying to avoid that topic. What I'm talking about here is your *health*. And yes, you can be skinny and unhealthy and you can be fat and healthy. So let's stick with the "healthy" and ignore the "fat."

Let me use myself as an example to make this point: Left to my own devices (and when I'm not being mindful and just going by rote) I will eat a whole lot of bread and other baked goods (especially cupcakes). I will eat lots of meat and drink plenty of cocktails and wine. Fruits and veggies? While I like them, I will declare them "too much work" and they get left by the wayside. What does this get me? Allergies, asthma, sore joints, fatigue, bad skin, and yes, excess weight.

I recently watched a movie that I found to be hugely inspirational. It's called *Fat, Sick, and Nearly Dead* (see Resources) and in short, it's about healing yourself with a plant-based diet. (It's free online, it's fabulous and funny, and you should go watch it right now.) I followed that diet for ten days and guess what went away? You got it, my allergies, asthma, sore joints, fatigue, bad skin, and eight pounds. By committing to eating the healthiest food I possibly could, I found that many of my chronic health conditions disappeared.

"Nutrition is huge—HUGE—for me. If I don't take time to eat right, I am grumpy. Things that don't seem to affect others affect me, so my son understands that at times I need to eat certain things, or ban things from the house (so I don't eat them)."

Oh, I forgot to mention something else: All that "clean" eating that made me feel great? It was really expensive and time-consuming as hell.

So, where does that leave me? It leaves me in the most challenging "middle ground"—an area of moderation and self-discipline. Do I want to give up coffee, cupcakes, and cocktails for the rest of my life? Hell, no. (In fact, tell me I can't ever have them again and I'll crave them like a mad junkie. I do not do well with absolutes. Some people do. I don't.) But having done the programs where I ate super clean for an extended period of time, I have also lived the rewards. I try very hard to be mindful of what I'm putting in my body, and to take full responsibility for it. What does that mean? That means nobody put a gun to my head and made me eat that cupcake. And when I eat that cupcake, I try to come at it with this approach:

1. Do I really want it?

2. How is it going to make me feel when I eat it?

3. How is it going to make me feel after I eat it?

4. Am I willing to accept the consequences that will come from ingesting this product? If yes, then

5. Enjoy the hell out of it.

Because, really, otherwise, why bother?

My friend Angie is a nutritionist. Angie loves cookies. She loves chocolate. And she eats them. I sometimes feel sorry for her when we're out in public, because people get pretty wiggy about eating in front of a nutritionist. We'll be at parties or at events, and someone will reach for a cookie on a tray and say "Oh, I know, I know, I really shouldn't be eating this." At her. For her benefit. Or theirs. I don't even know, it's some sort of weird projection-y self-conscious thing. I want to smack them. Angie is much more magnanimous than that. In fact, she usually says something like "Why not?" and grabs a cookie for herself.

REALITY CHECK:

Don't think in terms of "bad" foods and "good" foods. Food does not possess these qualities. Food simply exists. Some foods are more nutritious, and some foods are less nutritious. Try to eat more of the nutritious kind, and less of the non-nutritious kind.

What you do 20% of the time doesn't matter. It's what you do 80% of the time that matters. I really like this statement because it spits in the face of black and white thinking. No more "*Oooh, I'm such a bad person for eating this piece of cake.*" Are you eating cake 80% of the time? No? Then let yourself off the hook. Cake is yummy. *Enjoy* cake.

"Even though I'm thoughtful about what I put in my body I'm not rigid. There is no 'good' or 'bad' food, there is just food. Yes there are times that I could make healthier choices but I'm okay with that."

THE SOLUTION:

Here are my three tips for paying attention to what you put in your body.

1. MINDFUL EATING

Do you multi-task when you eat? Read the paper? Eat standing up? Eat at your desk while you do more work? Eat in the car? (I was recently on a trip overseas where we spent time with a wonderful English expatriate who travels all over Europe and Asia who makes a living as a food photographer. I don't remember how the topic came up, but we somehow started talking about cup holders in cars. He didn't seem to understand. "You mean you drink your coffee in the car?" he asked, incredulous. We, in turn, were incredulous that he was incredulous. The more we elaborated, explaining that we even had "travel mugs" in America which were designed so that our coffee could fit more easily into the cup holders in the car, the more he was convinced we were pulling his leg. "Of all the odd things we Americans do," we said, "*this* is the one you think is weird?" He had spent his life in Europe, where cafés abound, and if you want a cup of coffee, you go to the café, sit down, and order one. You may not stay long at all, but you sit down and drink it. To drink it in the car was completely strange to him. Perhaps as weird as we might think it would be to have cup holders in the shower. I started to tell him about fast food that was designed for easier eating-while-driving but at that point it looked like his head would explode, so I stopped.)

Here's an exercise whose difficulty might surprise you: Set a place at your table. Placemat, plate, utensils. Get out the good stuff. Use real cloth napkins, if you have them. Maybe a nice flower in a little vase. Then make yourself something delicious to eat. Sit down at the fancy table you've set—and eat. No multi-tasking. No reading. No telephone. No TV. Just you and your food. Take a good look at the food. How it shines, or doesn't. Its colors. How your knife or spoon carves or scoops through it. Bring it up to your nose and take a big whiff. How does it smell? Now—slowly—put it in your mouth. Close your eyes and inhale. (Much of our sense of taste is actually smell, and if you inhale slowly while the food is in your mouth, you will experience more of the aroma.) Put down your utensils. Now chew it … slowly. Experience the texture. Let it roll around on your tongue. Keep your attention entirely focused, as best you can, on the experience at hand. Now swallow, feeling it go down your throat and land in your stomach. Take a deep breath. Exhale.

This is mindful eating.

It's hard, isn't it? Did you find this exercise uncomfortable? Or was it relaxing and soothing to let go of everything else and just "be" with your food and your body? Mindfulness, the art of being as completely *present* (focused and attentive) for what is happening in and around us, is a spiritual practice that requires a great deal of discipline. When I say "pay attention to what you put in your body," I'm not just talking about not eating junk food. I'm talking about this.

Do I recommend eating like this all of the time? No. We are not monks or nuns. We are moms, and we have a lot of stuff on our plates (Ha!). But every once in a while, stopping and doing this can be a really informative exercise. It may uncover some interesting data: *I'm uncomfortable being alone* or *Wow, I really tend to rush through my food without tasting it* or *When I slow down and really enjoy my food, I eat a lot less.* It's worth a try.

2. KEEP A FOOD JOURNAL

Ever kept a food journal? It's basically where you keep track of everything you eat. You write down what you ate, when you ate it, and how much of it.

True confession time: *I hate keeping food journals!*

That said, I am well aware of their value. Simply put, they let you see in black and white (or blue and white or pink and blue ... knock yourself out with those gel pens, ladies) what you're actually eating vs. what you *think* you're eating. I have been truly astonished by some of the discrepancies I've seen in my diet when I've been really honest with my food journal. (And please, if you're going to do this, be honest. Hide it someplace where no one else can see, if you're embarrassed, but for Lord's sake, tell *yourself* the truth, won't you?) Those veggies and fruits were just not getting in as regularly as I told everyone (and myself) that they were. Ouch! Cold hard truth! Food journaling can also be a great way to uncover any food sensitivities you might have, especially if you track symptoms along with food. "Hmm, on those days I screamed at my kids for an hour straight, I hadn't eaten any breakfast!" or "Gee, on those nights when I had panic attacks, I had consumed five cups of coffee by the end of the day." Cause – effect. It's written out for you to see, and to decide whether you are ready to make some changes. In the Resources section in the back of this book I've included some information on tools that can help you keep track of these things.

3. ENJOY WHAT YOU EAT

For me, personally, this is the most important tip. I'm of French heritage, and my French heritage says that food is as much about pleasure as it is about fuel.

Nutrition studies have been conducted where scientists measured absorption of nutrients in people who were happy to be eating versus those who weren't, and guess what? Yep. When you were happy and enjoying your food, you get more nutrients out of it. Scientists have spoken about "the French Paradox" for years, trying to figure out why the culture that regularly eats cheese, wine and foie gras doesn't suffer from obesity nearly at the rates as our culture. There have been many guesses: They walk everywhere, it's the resveratrol in the red wine, etc. I'm sure it all adds up but I believe one of the main reasons is this: The French take mealtime *very* seriously. Go to any small town in France at lunchtime and most of the shops will be closed. One sits at a table, one prepares the food with care, and one enjoys their repast slowly and with pleasure. When mealtime is over, work can resume, but to do both at the same time is both uncivilized and unhealthy, in the French point of view, and I agree. Life is too short to eat bad food poorly. Or to eat poor food badly. If you can't sit down, look that food in the eye (ok, your eye, not the food's eye) and truly say "I enjoy this," then what's the point?

GET TO THE POINT:

- Pay attention to what you eat.
- Don't eat things that make you feel guilty.
- If it's going to go in your mouth, make sure to thoroughly enjoy it.

CHAPTER SIX
ASK FOR HELP

"I don't like to burden others with what I should be doing."

"I am an island unto myself. I loathe asking for help and do it only if left no other choice."

"There's a Superwoman complex I find I have in common with lots of other moms where I take on too much, try to handle it all, and make it look easy even when I am struggling. I have to really be close to drowning to ask for help."

"I have no problem asking for help (and providing it in return). And I'll be very specific about what I need, be it childcare, food, etc. I just went through a major family crisis, and there is no way I would have made it through w/out help."

THE PROBLEM:
Societal pressures, cultural shifts, and our own egos tell us that we "should" be able to "do it all." This leads to stress, isolation, and burnout.

As I surveyed and chatted up moms, I already knew that the chapter about food would be a potent topic. Food and women? Fuggedaboudit. And I knew the sleep topic would practically write itself. Moms are always tired. But this chapter? This one surprised me. I got answers I wasn't expecting. I also got some great insight and really powerful lessons on what it means to ask for help.

As moms, we tend to think we should be able to do it all ourselves. Well, at least in modern American culture we do.

Did you know that at the turn of the previous century, it was considered perfectly normal for middle-class families to have household help? Perhaps someone to help with the housework or the cooking. The farther you moved up the income ladder the more help you had, but even an average middle-class household might have a cook or a housekeeper. It wasn't considered a luxury, really. It was socially understood that keeping a house and raising a family required a great deal of work that was more than one person could usually handle.

I have a friend who was born in South Africa, had her children there, and then moved to the United States while they were still young. She does not work outside of the home, and she hires nannies to help with her children. She was astonished when some of the other moms in the neighborhood raised an eyebrow at this. Where she comes from, it's completely normal and expected to have nannies. But here in America, it's only something people do if they're terribly wealthy and they work outside of the home.

Our society lauds and jokes about the moms who "do it all." We're taught to strive for "having it all." We're tired. We're bedraggled.

"Before I had kids, I used to scoff at moms who went to the grocery store looking like shit. Why couldn't they be bothered to put themselves together? Now I get it. I'm lucky if I can get a comb through my hair before I go."

Here's the truth: You can't do it all by yourself. It's unrealistic to try. Until relatively recently in our nation's history, mothers had household help, and had their family around them to help raise their children. Grandmas, aunts, cousins, and sisters all gathered 'round and pitched in (sometimes under the same roof) to tend to the daily necessities of life. Now with our modern, mobile society, it's not at all unusual for kids to grow up living thousands of miles away from their grandparents and cousins. (Mine did.) This leaves the parents to have to scramble to find sitters, handle the housework, and do the cooking. And let's face it, that parent is usually the mom.

But this chapter isn't about housework. It's about asking for help with anything you need because you're human and you can't do it all. Perhaps you need someone to trade babysitting with you so you can work that extra shift, or you're caring for a sick parent and you need some help getting dinner on the table. Perhaps you think you might be suffering from depression and you're not sure what to do about it.

"I ought to be able to handle this," you tell yourself. "I don't want to be a burden to others."

REALITY CHECK:

You stink at asking for help. Is it really because you "don't want to be a burden to others" or is it that your pride and ego don't want to admit that you are a vulnerable human who can't do it all?

THE SOLUTION:

HOW TO ASK FOR HELP

1) BE BRAVE ABOUT BEING VULNERABLE –
When I polled moms and asked them about how good they were with asking for help, a great many of them said they didn't do it. Here's where the surprising part came in: Several moms said that they had tried asking for help, were rebuffed, and made it a policy not to ask again.

To be clear, I did not ask these moms what their specific asks were about. I don't know them personally.

I also don't doubt the reality of asking for help and being flat-out turned down. I know it can happen.

But then I saw this:

"Asking others for help opens a door to reciprocity and selflessness. There is a relationship there to vulnerability. And I hate that."

There it is.

Whatever those women asked for, and were ultimately disappointed in the outcome, they were in a vulnerable position when they asked. And to be denied when one is vulnerable *hurts*. And rather than risk being hurt again, they closed off their hearts.

Being hurt and risking a "no" is a chance we take when we ask for help.

Asking for help can be hard. It requires you to have some humility. It requires you to admit that you aren't perfect at everything and that you have a limited capacity. It requires you to admit that you are fallible and human. As moms in this day and age, we're asked to do a lot. And we do it. We love, nurse, clean, comfort, work, organize, drive, kiss, hug, and straighten. Be that as it may, we're not always the right person for the job.

Let's turn this "I should be able to handle this" thought process around.

"I've had chapters in my life where others sacrifice in serving me and my family allowed for us to thrive when it would have otherwise been a battlefield instead of a joyous time. Allowing others to love on me through service is an amazing thing."

Asking for help opens up the opportunity for someone to be of service.

2) LOOSEN THE CONTROL REINS –

"We need to ask for help when needed. We need to let go of the control."

We're the mom, right? It's our title. We're proud of it. We're good at it. *Nobody can do it as well as we can.*

Sister, you gotta let that go.

Classic example: Couple has a baby. Mom complains to Dad, "I need you to help more with the baby! I'm tired! Could you please just *step up?*" Dad steps up. Mom goes out for the day, gets some time alone. Then she comes home and criticizes how the child is dressed, what activities were done, and how the whole day went down. Dad is discouraged and withdraws, again. Lather, rinse, and repeat.

I once had a mom tell me (with a perverse kind of pride) that she had never had an evening away from her 8- and 9-year-old children, because "I don't trust *anyone* to take care of them properly."

That way madness lies.

No one can care for your children like you do. It's true. No one can clean your house to your exact specifications. Quite possible. No one can possibly understand your complicated and specific life problems to the degree you understand them. Maybe. But here's the thing: There are people who can do all of these things *well enough* and once you are willing to trust them with that responsibility, your life is going to get much easier.

3) HIRE YOUR WEAKNESSES – I was listening to an interview with the female CEO of a wildly successful company. When asked for her #1 business tip, she said "Hire your weaknesses." You're the CEO of your family. Figure out what you're not good at (or flat out don't want to do) and delegate those responsibilities. Instead of feeling embarrassed or ashamed of not being good at something, try understanding that some people specialize in that thing you're not good at and they're waiting for you to call upon them to help.

Ever have something like this happen? You're talking to a friend, asking them where they were all weekend, and they say something like this, "Oh, I was stuck at home making pies. I promised it for the school auction. I hate making pies! It took me all weekend!"

You love making pies, and you're good at it. "WHY DIDN'T YOU CALL ME?" you wail. "I was sitting at home all weekend. I could have helped you!"

"Oh, I didn't want to bother you."

It's like that.

We moms say we don't ask for help for a lot of reasons:

"I didn't want to bother you."

"I ought to be able to do this by myself."

"I was embarrassed to ask."

You think everyone is in the same boat, too busy or overwhelmed to add anyone else's problems to their to-do list. But it doesn't always work that way. You can find people out there who want to help you. Who are waiting to help. But they have no idea you need their help. Because you didn't ask.

A close friend of mine who's a single mom recently found herself in an unfortunate situation where she needed a new place to live and a great many new house furnishings in a fairly short period of time. My suggestion to her? "Put it on Facebook. Tell your friends what's going on." This rattled some other members of her family, who counseled her that it was a bad idea "We don't air our personal business like that." She did it anyway. Guess what? Her friends rallied around her, gifting her with a very good deal on a new place to live, and plenty of household items that they were happy to donate to support their dear friend. When my friend was willing to show her vulnerability and ask for help, she received it.

4) BE SPECIFIC ABOUT WHAT YOU NEED – Part of the reason my friend was so successful in getting what she needed was she was very specific in what she asked for. "We need a two bedroom rental in [her area]." "We need a child's bed." This allowed her friends to know precisely how they could help her.

(NOTE TO HELPERS: "Let me know if there's anything I can do" is a phrase we often put out to friends who are hurting or in need, and we may even mean it, but being specific with your offer is even better: "I know you're in bed recovering from your surgery. I would like to prepare dinners for your family. I can bring them over tomorrow night and put them in your freezer. May I do that for you?" Trust me, it helps.)

GET TO THE POINT:

- Asking for help requires acknowledging vulnerability and imperfection.
- Letting go of control allows us more freedom and peace.
- Consider which things are difficult/challenging/distasteful for you to do and find someone whom you can pay/barter/trade with to do the job instead.
- Be specific about what you need help with.

CHAPTER SEVEN
GET TOUCHED

"It's easier to not have touch....so that a person doesn't get too close to you. They might see your weaknesses."

THE PROBLEM:
Our touch-starved lives lead to higher stress, more illness, and social animosity.

Quick trivia question: What's the largest organ in the human body?

Your liver? Good guess. That's a big one. Your small intestine? Another good guess. That sucker is all curled up in there, and is surprisingly long when you lay it flat and measure it end to end (I don't recommend you do this). But the real answer is: your skin. Take it all off, lay it out, and measure it and it would be about twenty-two square feet. Weigh it and you'd find on average is weighs about twenty pounds. (Again, don't try this at home. Just take my word for it.)

How often do you think about your skin? Maybe if you do at all it's your face and your arms; the parts that you show to the world. You may think about whether it's clean, or smooth, or dimpled—you know, *appearance* stuff. But the appearance of your skin is just the surface.

Our skin is an extraordinary organ, which does so much more than just keep our guts from falling out. (Which would have been enough.) It is the big gun of our immune system, serving not only as a physical barrier to pathogens but also containing an acid mantle (fancy word for the pH of your skin) that discourages pathogens. Our skin is waterproof, breathable, and self-cleaning (take *that*, Gore-Tex'). Just a few of the other purposes it serves include temperature regulation (the phrase *sweating like a pig* is weird because pigs don't really sweat ... that's why they lie around in mud, to cool off. So, the next time you're soaking through that $100 silk blouse, consider the alternative), a regulator of blood pressure, and synthesizer of Vitamin D (Vitamin D would probably be better named Hormone D, since we mostly synthesize it ourselves). But the main reason we are all gathered here today, dearly beloved, is to talk about the skin's wonderful purpose as a *mediator of touch*.

Touch. Of the main five senses it can be argued that touch is easily the most important. ***Our sense of touch is how we relate to the world.*** Think about that for a minute. I'll wait.

OK, I'm back.

Still need convincing? Think about what you're doing right now. You're probably sitting down as you read this. Can you feel your rear end in the chair or sofa as you read this? (If you can't, GO FOR A WALK AND READ THIS LATER! YOUR BUTT HAS FALLEN ASLEEP!) The parts of your body that are touching the chair? How about your back? Is it touching the chair? Is it not? Where are your feet? Are they on the ground? Are you propping them up? Every point where your body is touching something else is a point where your sense of touch is being stimulated. The chair. Your clothes. Your glasses. Your hands on the keyboard (or paper if you're reading this printed out). Our minds are taking in thousands of points of data in any given second. It filters the vast majority out (so we don't go crrrraaaazzzzyyy), but right now I'd like you to take a moment and let some of it back in. We're going to do the same exercise as we did above, but this time we're really going to *focus*.

Sit back, close your eyes, and take a few deep breaths. Lay down any extraneous thoughts or worries you're nursing right now (you can pick them up again in three minutes). After a few more deep breaths, let your focus go to your body as it is right now. We're going for sensation, here. Specifically, touch. As we did a moment ago, feel your seat. (Not with your hands, that's for a later chapter.) Just experience the sensation of your rear end on the cushion. Is it soft? Hard? Are you sitting on a wooden chair? On the floor? Now your feet. Are they flat on the floor? Dangling? Are you wearing shoes? If so, where are you feeling your shoes touch your feet? Now your shoulders: Are they tight? Loose? Are you wearing heavy clothing? A scratchy sweater? Is there a zipper? Can you (again, without using your hands) feel the metal of the zipper against your skin? How 'bout a bra? Are you wearing one? Can you feel the underwire, or the elastic?

OK, *abracadabra*, come out of your trance.

All of that sensation you just had? All of the parts where you felt your skin touching something? That was your sense of touch at work. And guess what? The parts where you didn't feel something touching are also your sense of touch at work. They were (and still are, if you're not dead yet) reading the air temperature, whether or not there was a breeze, the fact that they were not covered with clothing. When you get up and walk across the room, your sense of touch is still at work, determining where you are in space, the pressure with which you hit the floor, when to roll your foot to take the next step, and more. Multiple sensory cells in your skin work to determine all of these things, all of the time.

Imagine living without your sense of smell. Bummer, right? You couldn't smell flowers, or fresh-baked bread. (You couldn't taste most things, either, because your sense of smell is a huge part of what you think your sense of taste is.)

OK, now lose your sense of taste. Also a bummer. No salty, sweet, or bitter.

No sense of hearing? Highly undesirable. No music, no lilt of your lover's voice, no children's laughter.

No sight? Augh! No colors. No seeing smiles. No beautiful landscapes.

Yet we all know or know of people who get along quite well in life without these senses. Do you know anyone living without his or her sense of touch? Diabetes, Multiple Sclerosis, and several other diseases can impair the sense of touch. Due to rare conditions, some people are even born with no sense of touch whatsoever. In any case, loss of lack of touch is very dangerous. Usually because those who suffer from this condition have a tendency to not be able to tell when they're injured.

So hopefully now we've established that our sense of touch is a terribly important one, and one that we take for granted. But did you know your body requires touch? That it's wired for touch? That you actually have a daily requirement for touch?

> ## REALITY CHECK:
> YOU NEED TO BE TOUCHED. Healthy, safe, physical contact is a vital part of your health as a human being.

How much touch is enough? Well, that's like asking how much nutrition is enough. I'll begin this topic by explaining what studies have shown happens when we don't receive touch. Interestingly, the bulk of this research has been done on two main populations: newborns, and the elderly (apparently all of us in between are too hard to catch).

TOUCH FOR BABIES

The first study has to do with babies who were failing to thrive in certain Eastern European orphanages. The babies were being fed, were given medicine, and were generally being cared for. Or so they thought. Yet these babies were failing to thrive. They were small. They were sickly. Many of them were even dying. What was going wrong?

They weren't being held.

For various reasons (low staffing, cultural setting, etc.) these babies spent the vast majority of their time alone in their cribs. They would be touched when it came time for feeding, diapering, etc, but that was it. Once these babies began to be held, cuddled, rocked, stroked – *touched* – they got better. They gained weight.

Ever noticed how much a mama cat licks her kittens? Licks 'em like crazy. There's a reason for it. If she doesn't, they die. They need all sorts of tactile stimulation for their bodies to begin performing the functions they need to survive.

Rats. Baby rats. Mama rats lick their babies like crazy, too. Scientists separated the baby rats from their mama (but still fed them). Guess what? They died. In another variant of the test, they separated the rats but this time they stroked them with a little paintbrush (scientists are weird). Guess what? The rats that got stroked regularly with the little brush fared much better than the baby rats who didn't get touched at all. Touch isn't just something nice. Touch is vital.

OK, so, that's for babies. Developing neurons and all that jazz. What about the other end?

TOUCH FOR THE ELDERLY

The elderly, particularly in our touch-phobic American culture, tend not to get touched as often. Why? Lots of reasons. Isolation. Elder-phobia. Cultural mores against touch. Studies have been done with this demographic as well. Guess what? When elderly people receive comforting pats on the back, massage, backrubs, hugs, have their hands held, etc., their anxiety levels decrease. Their immune systems improve. Their blood pressure lowers. Their reported happiness increases.

TOUCH FOR YOU

So, we know that touch is vital for the health and well-being of newborns. And we know that touch is vital for the health and well-being of the elderly. *Isn't it probably a safe bet to assume that it's also vital for the health and well-being of everyone in between?* Most of the research on this age group has been done under the umbrella of massage therapy. In the interest of space, I'll cut to the chase: Research studies have proven that massage therapy can:

- Alleviate pain

- Enhance immunity

- Improve range-of-motion

- Lessen depression and anxiety

- Reduce post-surgery adhesions and swelling

- and much more

Hopefully you now see why it's so darned important that you receive healthy touch as often as you can. In our touch-phobic culture, this can be a challenge. But I've got a few suggestions here that will hopefully set you down the path to getting touched:

THE SOLUTION:

1 - GET MASSAGE

This one's obvious. Go get a professional massage. You can choose from many, many different styles of massage, but the vast majority offered will be called a Swedish style or relaxation massage. These are the most common and the modality that most people are trained in. Never had a professional massage before? Here's what you can expect:

You will be taken to a room with a massage table (it looks sort of like a cross between a bed and something you'd see in a doctor's office). Your massage therapist should ask you about your health. Be sure to mention any surgeries, injuries, rashes or anything else in your health history. This can and will have an impact on the sort of work they do on you. Yes, it matters. A good massage intake form will have these questions written right on it for you.

If it's your first time, be sure to tell that to the massage therapist as well. They will be able to talk you through what's going on and what to expect.

The massage therapist will ask what areas are bothering you and what you'd like work on today. It's entirely fine to say "No particular areas. I'm here for relaxation." They will then leave then tell you how they'd like you to position yourself on the table "We'll start you face up. Or let's start face down." If they don't you can either:

a) ask,

or

b) just start face down (that's how most massage practitioners start).

They will then leave the room. At this point, you will be expected to undress down to the point where you're comfortable. Normally this means down to just underpants or entirely nude. You will then get under the sheets, just like you were getting into bed, and cover yourself up. The practitioner will then knock on the door, ask if you're ready, and return to the room.

Here's why you are asked to undress: Most massage is done on bare skin using oil or lotion to facilitate "glide." This allows the massage practitioner to best feel what your tissues (muscles, tendons, skin, etc.) are doing, and also gives you the most direct and beneficial massage. A professional and ethical massage therapist will always keep the areas they are not working on draped and will be sure that your modesty is preserved and your private areas (genitals, "gluteal cleavage" i.e. your butt crack, and breasts for women) are never exposed. When it's time for you to lie on your back, the sheets will be used to cover your chest.

Some people opt to keep their underwear on, others take everything off. The massage therapist will usually know which you have chosen simply by feeling it through the sheets and either choice is fine.

If, after knowing about the reasons why massage is best done on bare skin, and knowing that professional and ethical boundaries dictate you will be kept covered, you still don't feel comfortable disrobing, let the massage therapist know this. While it might not be as effective or might not be what they're used to, a massage can still be delivered through clothing. (Without the oil, of course.) I tell my clients the choice is theirs (after explaining everything I've explained here to you). Nearly every one of them chooses to disrobe after they've been told what to expect and why it's suggested.

Once you're on the table and covered up, the MT will make sure you're comfortable and may add pillows or bolsters under your legs or arms as needed. The goal is for you to be super-comfy so you can relax. (This also makes less work for them, as a relaxed body is much easier to massage than a tense one.) They will then undrape the area they plan to work on, apply lotion, and massage that area using strokes, squeezes, compressions, and rocking. This will be done to as many areas as the session has time for. Once done, the massage therapist will let you know that time is up. They will leave the room, and then you will uncover yourself, get dressed, and head out. Go slowly! Your blood pressure is likely to have decreased and you might feel a bit "massage drunk" from the deep relaxation. Yay, you!

You will find many, many massage therapists practicing out there. Finding a good one, who really listens to you and knows your body, can sometimes involve a bit of searching. Don't be discouraged if your first session wasn't to your liking. He or she is out there! A good place to look online is through the professional organizations. (See the Resources section of this book.)

Once people learn how beneficial massage can be, the bigger challenge isn't whether or not to do it, but how to afford it. The good news is, more expensive isn't always better. (You can find so-so MTs at the deluxe spas, and terrific MTs working part-time out of their homes.) Check around for prices.

Another great way to get some affordable massage: Make friends with a massage student! They're required to do lots and lots of practice hours while they're in school. You'd not only be helping them, but you'd be getting some free massage. Finally, find out when your local massage school has student clinics. Once the students reach a certain degree of aptitude, they're then allowed to practice (with supervision) on the general public. The rates here are usually very affordable. Once you've realized the benefits of massage, you won't see it as a "luxury." It's really maintenance.

A question I often get is "How much massage should I get?" My answer? As much as you can afford! But here's what I really think (it's sort of a thing we massage therapists tell each other): A massage every two weeks is a great goal to shoot for. (Every week is even better, but bi-weekly still gets a gold star.)

2 - BECOME A HUGGER

We're pretty touch-phobic in our culture. There have been studies done on the cultural norms for "personal space." Guess which country's people have the largest requirement for personal space? USA! USA! Yep, don't fence us in. In fact, don't stand so close to me. (OK, that's The Police. They're two-thirds British, which is a culture that doesn't like to touch much, either.) In the test, they had a person walk toward the subject and had the subject say "stop" when they got uncomfortable with how close the other person was. Americans like a good eighteen inches of personal space around them.

I've noticed this cultural difference a lot when I've traveled. I was in the Vatican museum in Rome, on a hot summer day, and a huge group from Korea came through at the same time we were there. Time after time, I felt myself being crowded and my personal space being invaded as we moved along. I felt myself growing angry at their rudeness, and then I checked myself. They weren't being rude. That part of the world is very heavily populated and they simply don't have the huge foot-and-a-half personal space requirements that Americans have. It was perfectly ok where they came from to cram in tight to get a look at a painting in public.

While the English measured slightly closer than Americans in their personal space bubbles, they still aren't a particularly touch-friendly culture. Ever been to England? They apologize like mad if they accidently touch you! It's kind of funny, really.

Less funny is the story of my friend from South Africa. She moved to the US about ten years ago, and immediately found that people were uneasy when she would hug or stroke their children. "Back in Africa, everybody hugs and holds each other's kids," she said. "I thought nothing of it. But I had to learn to stop doing that here in America because people got really uncomfortable." She loves America, by the way. She finds the people here actually warmer and more open than folks back home, as a rule. But the touching part? Not so much.

So, in our culture where we like lots of personal space, where we get freaked out if someone stands too close to us, where we're constantly bombarded by the fear-mongering media of stories of child molesters and predators, how do we get MORE touch?

We start touching others.

An interesting phenomenon is happening in schools. It wasn't there when I was in high school. Kids hug. A lot. The high-schoolers hug each other. Boys hug girls, girls hug girls, boys hug boys hello, good-bye, wishing them success, when someone wins a game, when someone's sad, etc. This was not done when I was in high school in the early 1980s. Some touch-specialists theorize that this increase in hugging is a direct result of the child-molestation fears which swept through the country in the 1980s. This resulted in schools instructing all teachers and instructors not to touch their students in any way, lest their gestures are misconstrued as sexually inappropriate and they be sued. So, the theory goes, the students, hungry for that warm and friendly touch to their arm, pats on the back, and congratulatory hugs from their teachers, have since turned to each other for that basic human contact. Interesting, huh?

I've also noticed a lot more hugging in social and even business circles than I remember there being twenty years ago. And I am *for* it. Studies have shown that cultures that touch more are more peaceful and less aggressive than cultures that do not. (This isn't an America vs. Everyone Else thing, either. They've found these differences existing in cultures around the world. More touch = less war.)

So, become a hugger. Or a pat-on-the-back-er. Or an arm-toucher. Here's the cool thing about it: Giving touch has nearly the same benefits as receiving touch. Remember that exercise we did at the beginning where we closed our eyes and focused on what we could feel touching our skin and what we couldn't? Touch works both ways.

I was in a massage class, learning a technique called lymphatic drainage. It's a very light, very lovely, incredibly relaxing technique that involves rhythmic stroking and light stretching of the skin. The technique is known to have sometimes dramatic results in lowering blood pressure on the spot. But guess what? *It's also been shown to lower the blood pressure of the people who give it.* How crazy is that? I already have low blood pressure, and at one point when I was practicing the technique on someone else I had to go lie down and put my feet up. I had lowered my own blood pressure too much just by *giving* the appropriate touch.

So, when you hug someone, or when you rub their shoulders, or pat their hand, you are not only giving someone the gift of touch, but you're getting it in return. (But please, be socially appropriate. The goal here is to calm and relax people, not to give instructions on How To Be a Creep.)

3 - TAKE A TOUCH(Y) CLASS

But Leslie, you say. I am all alone! I have no one to touch or to touch me. Well, I say to you. Do not despair. Go to school! Or, at least, take a class. You have many touch-oriented classes available to you. Massage schools will often offer classes to laypeople who aren't necessarily looking to become massage therapists themselves, but would like to know how to give a massage to a friend or loved one. Partner yoga is where you're paired up with someone who helps you stretch. Plenty of touching there, plus the benefits of yoga! How 'bout a dance class? Particularly, ballroom, salsa, or any partner dancing. Nope, you don't have to go with someone. You can go alone and will be partnered. And you will get amazing exercise. Again, what's not to like?

Shy about touching someone you don't know in these classes? I get it. Here's the funny thing though: after a while, you get really used to it. When I started massage school, we pretty much had to go right to it, putting our hands on strangers (who were *naked* under those sheets!) and practicing our (then very awkward) moves on them. It's amazing how quickly shyness melts away when you've got a common goal and a ton of stuff to learn together. Massage school definitely made me a "toucher." In fact, I sometimes have to check myself and realize "Ok, Les, not everyone is as comfortable with touch as you are. You might want to *ask* them before you put your hands on 'em!"

4 - HAVE SEX

What's more touch-centric than sex? It's such a central part of touch that it often causes a lot of confusion in our culture. Sexual relations are one of the main ways that adults in our society receive touch. Nothing wrong with that, except it's also one of the *only* ways adults in our culture receive touch. This can lead to a great many mixed/confused signals as to what constitutes non-sexual touch. It certainly hasn't helped things by having some prostitution rings front as "massage parlors." This confusion also leads to many people being uncomfortable receiving massage, especially from a male therapist, as they fear that there will somehow be a sexual component to it. Whether they fear it will be in their minds or the practitioners' minds, I don't know, but it's truly a shame. Some of the very best, most professional and most talented massage therapists I know are men.

But I digress. Sexual confusion aside, having sex is a lovely way to get more touch into your life. Many of the benefits of sex (relaxation, reduced anxiety, strengthening of relationships) can be traced directly to the touch aspects of it. An interesting note: Couples who seek out sex therapists when they're having dysfunction in their sexual relationship are often surprised to find that one of the first things the therapist tells them to do is to stop having intercourse. For the first few weeks, their "homework" often consists of simply getting back to the touching part of the act, exploring each other's skin and re-igniting the pleasure derived simply from that.

Plus, an orgasm releases oxytocin, which is a lovely hormone in our bodies that makes us all calm and cozy. WIN-WIN!

Got no one to have sex with? Yes you do. Yourself! (More on that ... now.)

5 - TOUCH YOURSELF

Yes, I mean what you think I mean, but I also mean a lot more. Let's save the sexual part for last (dessert!), and talk about a few other ways you can touch yourself:

1) WEAR SENSUAL FABRIC – Silky. Soft. Fuzzy. What are the kinds of fabric you love to feel on your body? For me it's cashmere. Warm and cozy and sensuously soft at the same time, it's a fabric that makes me feel fabulous. I love the way it feels on my skin, and I love to run my hands over it as I'm wearing it. How bout you? Silk? Satin? If it's not clothing, perhaps it's in your bedding? Ever slept on satin sheets? Oooh! Your touch receptors will go mad!

2) BATHS – Baths are a wonderful way to treat your skin to some more stimulation. Most of us hop in the shower and take care of our ablutions as expeditiously as possible. But a nice soak in a warm bath (hot baths are actually a stressor to the body), maybe with a lovely sea-sponge or a scrub brush. How 'bout a bath fizz bomb or some Jacuzzi bubbles? Now we're talkin'! Skin stimulation galore.

3) DRY BRUSHING – Dry brushing involves taking a soft bath brush and using it dry on dry skin (i.e., not in the shower or bath). Using very light strokes, brush your skin toward the direction of your heart. Not only will this help exfoliate, and improve your lymphatic circulation, but it will also be stimulating all of those touch receptors in your body. Dry-brushing is a very healthy habit. And remember, light touch. Less is more. (If you use much pressure, you're not getting the lymphatic benefits.)

1) MASTURBATION – C'mon, did you think I was going to leave this out? No way. Touching ourselves sexually is a delightful way to feel good all over. We don't need to wait for someone else to get touched "in that way," Far from being a last resort, masturbation allows us to know ourselves intimately, and to receive physical pleasure as we need to. Out of practice? Never done it? Need a little help? You can learn good

techniques from some terrific websites which are female-friendly and have a healthy outlook on sex. (See the Resources section of this book.) You can also now find a trove of websites that offer sex materials for religious couples. Take a look! If you can think of it, it exists on the Internet.

In conclusion, please know that "touch" can be thought about in so many different ways—not just as it relates to sex. Skin is what you're in, and it does so much for us. When we take the time to love it back, and really show it that we know it, the health and wellness benefits are manifold. Happy touching!

GET TO THE POINT:

- Our sense of touch is how we interact with the world.
- Receiving regular, healthy touch lowers blood pressure, boosts immunity, and reduces anxiety.
- Massage, hugs, partner dancing, stroking a pet, and sex are some of the ways we can receive more touch in our lives.

AFTERWORD

So here we are, at the end of the book. If you've read this far, you've learned my tips for self-care. I hope you find them helpful. I hope they bring you some peace and rejuvenation. I also hope they *don't* lead you to feel as though this is going to help you lead a more balanced life.

Screw "balance." I hate that word.

Balance strikes me as a terribly precarious thing. I imagine one of those old balance scales; you know, the ones with the two plates that you have put absolutely equal amounts of stuff on to get the arrow on the scale to balance just right? One tiny bit more on one side or the other, and the scale is no longer balanced.

What do we mean by balance, anyway? That we spend 50% of our time at work and 50% with family? 25% on self care, 25% on family, 25% on school, and 25% volunteering?

Life simply doesn't work that way.

I have a trick I do in my seminars to prove this point: I ask the participants to stand, then show them a yoga pose that involves standing on one foot while wrapping the other leg around the standing one. The arms are wound around each other as well. It's called *garudasana* or "eagle pose" and it's very challenging to one's balance. I notice a lot stumbling and wobbling and giggling when this happens, because it's difficult.

I look around the room, and I find the person who's doing it with the most confidence. (I always find one yoga person in the room who puts out the "Ha! I've GOT this!" vibe when I do this exercise.) I walk up to that person and I say "HURRICANE!" and I push them out of the pose. (I do it gently so as not to hurt them. I don't need to get sued.)

Imagine trees during a hurricane. Some big, strong, tall oak trees snap right in half when the storm hits, and some soft, pliant willow trees bend in the face of the pressure, then bounce back.

The point is this: we can practice balance all we like, but we can't avoid hurricanes that come along and knock us off balance. Say a huge project comes up at work: Your "50 percent work/50 percent home" plans are going to have to fall by the wayside. They need you at work. Or let's say a family member gets very sick. Taking care of them is going to take up more of your time than you had planned. It's ok. That's how life works.

So, while balance is fine, and yoga balance poses are very good for you, I like to encourage cultivating *flexibility* and *resilience* first. Think willow tree, not oak.

Flexibility: How far can you bend when that hurricane hits?

Resilience: How readily can you bounce back after the hurricane has left?

THAT's what's going to help you manage stress.

And so I hope that the preceding seven tips I've offered in this book are taken in that spirit. The spirit of flexibility and resilience. Not as rigid templates that you must adhere to or you have somehow failed, but as safety nets you know will help you bend and bounce back when life's stresses come your way.

And remember: Life is a trip. Don't forget to pack your big girl panties.

ACKNOWLEDGEMENTS

Writing is a solitary experience. Making a book is not. I wish to express my heartfelt thanks to the following people (most of them moms!) for helping to make this book happen:

- Janica Smith, author's assistant extraordinaire, for being both the driver and the navigator of this bus.

- Jan King, publishing coach, for holding my hand at the beginning.

- Karen Lynn Maher, writing coach, for catching this baby at the end.

- Lauren Hidden, editor, for cleaning up my messes.

- Yvonne Park at www.pearcreative.ca, book designer, for making my words look like a book instead of a term paper.

- Betsy Talbot, friend who would help bury a body, for her terrifyingly honest critique. (She was right … *mostly*.)

- Jennifer Jefferies, ND, for putting me on the spot and starting this entire project.

- Sara Harvey Yao and Michele Lisenbury Christensen, for introducing me to "White Space Time"

- The Moms Who Talked: Sharice Belikoff, Lorinne Burke, Katie Frigon, Katie Holt, Sonia Michaels, Nina Mills, Betsy Moore, Anne Pillsbury, Rebecca Snyder Amanda Predmore, Kristin Ardery, Lisa Barger, Jessica Bryan, Laurel Geis, Debbie Dubrow, Rachel Seifert, Heather Irish and Jennifer Ziebarth. You did a sister a solid.

- Kate and Zach Evans, my kids, for being smart, funny, compassionate human beings and for keeping the asshattery to a minimum.

- Chris Evans, my husband and best friend. Your love, support, and oh-so-gentle placement of boot-in-ass were vital to this process. This book could not have happened without you, for many, many reasons. I love you madly.

RESOURCES

SLEEP

Sleep Hygiene
www.sleepfoundation.org
This site is very user-friendly and contains a great deal of helpful information about getting better sleep.

White Noise Machine
www.marpac.com
I use the Marpac Dohm-DS Dual Speed Sound Conditioner.

EXERCISE

Exercise Tracking
www.fitbit.com
I love my Fitbit! I have a Fitbit Flex which is a bracelet I wear on my arm 24/7 (except when I'm taking the 2-3 hours to charge it once a week). It measures the steps I take during the day, the calories I burn, how much sleep I get at night, and more. It has a terrific online user interface and even lets you link up with your friends to compare exercise notes.

Treadmill Desk
www.lifespanfitness.com
Some people rig up their own, or just buy a desk to cover the treadmill they already have, but I bought a brand new rig. I use the LifeSpan TR1200-DT

(2013 Model). I ordered it from Amazon.com. It comes mostly assembled.

WATER
Water Filtration
www.mavea.com
I'm a big fan of the Mavea brand of water filters. Attractive pitchers, easy to use, and they make my water taste great.

SPIRIT
Meditation
www.meditation.com
A good site for getting introduced to meditation. Contains some guided meditation videos.

NUTRITION
Fat, Sick and Nearly Dead
www.fatsickandnearlydead.com
Terrific documentary about a man who healed himself through a plant-based diet. Funny, down-to-earth, and inspiring.

Meal Tracking
www.myfitnesspal.com
The best online meal-tracking tool I've ever used. They crowd-source their database, so anytime something gets entered, it goes up in the system (and gets checked/confirmed by other users). Also can be used on your smartphone.

TOUCH
Massage

American Massage Therapy Association
www.amtamassage.org
Professional organization for licensed and certified massage therapists. Contains a "find a massage therapist" feature.

Associated Bodywork & Massage Professionals
www.abmp.org
Another professional organization for the industry.

Female-Positive Sex Toys

Eden Fantasys
www.edenfantasys.com
Thorough product reviews. Friendly owners. Great customer service.

Babeland
www.babeland.com
Seattle-based company. Very sex-positive. Down-to-earth. Strong community involvement.

ORGANIZATION *(While this topic wasn't addressed directly in this book, it couldn't have been written without the following):*
The Pomodoro Technique
www.pomodorotechnique.com
A productivity management technique developed by Francesco Cirillo in the late 1980s. It's a great focusing tool for those of us who suffer from "Mommy Brain."

Focus Time
www.focustimeapp.com
iPhone app that utilizes The Pomodoro Technique

Getting Things Done
www.davidco.com
Time management technique developed by David Allen.

Things for Mac
www.culturedcode.com/things
Mac, iPhone, iPad app that utitlizes the Getting Things Done method

NOTES

1   "Holmes and Rahe Stress Scale." *Wikipedia.* Wikimedia Foundation, 27 May 2013. Web. 17 June 2013.

2   "Brain Basics: Understanding Sleep." *: National Institute of Neurological Disorders and Stroke (NINDS).* N.p., n.d. Web. 21 June 2013.

3   "Hygiene" *Merriam-Webster.* Merriam-Webster, n.d. Web. 08 Apr. 2013.

4   Mann, Denise. "Alcohol and a Good Night's Sleep Don't Mix." *WebMD.* WebMD, 22 Jan. 2013. Web. 21 June 2013.

5   "Physical Activity and Health." *Centers for Disease Control and Prevention.* Centers for Disease Control and Prevention, 16 Feb. 2011. Web. 24 June 2013.

6   "Get Up. Get Out. Don't Sit." *The New York Times* *http://well.blogs.nytimes.com/2012/10/17/get-up-get-out-dont-sit*

7   www.leslieirishevans.com/42/multitasking-makes-you-stupid-by-debbie-rosemont